READY
TO
LEARN

THE **FRAME** MODEL
FOR OPTIMIZING
STUDENT SUCCESS

PEG GRAFWALLNER

Solution Tree | Press

a division of

Solution Tree

555 North Morton Street
Bloomington, IN 47404
800.733.6786 (toll free) / 812.336.7700
FAX: 812.336.7790

email: info@SolutionTree.com
SolutionTree.com

Visit **go.SolutionTree.com/instruction** to download the free reproducibles in this book.

Printed in the United States of America

Library of Congress Cataloging-in-Publication Data

Names: Grafwallner, Peggy J., 1960- author.
Title: Ready to learn : the FRAME model for optimizing student success /
  Peg Grafwallner.
Description: Bloomington, IN : Solution Tree Press, [2020] | Includes
  bibliographical references and index.
Identifiers: LCCN 2019016528 | ISBN 9781949539318
Subjects: LCSH: Effective teaching. | Lesson planning. | Classroom
  management.
Classification: LCC LB1025.3 .G69355 2020 | DDC 371.102--dc23
LC record available at https://lccn.loc.gov/2019016528

Solution Tree
Jeffrey C. Jones, CEO
Edmund M. Ackerman, President

Solution Tree Press
President and Publisher: Douglas M. Rife
Associate Publisher: Sarah Payne-Mills
Art Director: Rian Anderson
Managing Production Editor: Kendra Slayton
Senior Production Editors: Tara Perkins and Todd Brakke
Content Development Specialist: Amy Rubenstein
Copy Editor: Jessi Finn
Proofreader: Sarah Ludwig
Text and Cover Designer: Laura Cox
Editorial Assistant: Sarah Ludwig

Acknowledgments

This book began nearly three years ago as an idea scribbled in a notebook that eventually became a structured method of supporting teachers in the classroom. I could not have written this book without the help and support of the following.

Jackie Bladow, who was recommended to me as an excellent middle school resource teacher. (She is!) I am indebted to you for your time and talent in designing this awesome middle school lesson. Thank you, Jackie!

Tika Epstein, whom I met on Twitter, is without a doubt a kindred spirit. Tika's elementary lesson demonstrates her purpose and passion for her students and the greater good. I am so honored to have worked with Tika and can't wait to meet her in Vegas! I'm on my way, friend!

Abby Felten is a former colleague of mine and one of my favorite collaborators. Our collaboration has been successful because of our deep respect for the skills and talents of the other. The vocabulary lesson used for the Exemplary Classroom section in chapter 1 was one of our most successful lessons because it was an engaging, skill-based lesson. Thank you, Abby!

Joe Koester is one of the best humanities teachers I have had the pleasure to work with. Joe's dry sense of humor has made him a student favorite; this, along with the dedication to his craft, has made him an exemplary teacher in the few short years he's been teaching. Thank you, Joe, for allowing me to use this excellent lesson.

Mike Moore is a premier mathematics teacher who makes mathematics accessible and engaging. Mike's lessons are real, relevant, and relatable. His use of expert-stations lessons is one of the best lessons I have ever observed. Thank you, Mike, for all of your help.

Jessica Overland—thank you for reading and offering feedback. I appreciate you!

To Amy Rubenstein, my favorite writing coach. Amy helped me flesh out the ideas and make sure I was making sense. Every question she asked, every suggestion she made, brought us to this point. The lesson templates were genius! Thank you, Amy, for everything!

Finally, Tara Perkins, my former editor, and Todd Brakke, my current editor—thank you both for your editing finesse, patience, and flexibility in working with a novice author. Tara, your queries helped me to become a better writer. Todd, your ability to talk me off the ledge more than once and empower my confidence cannot be overlooked. Thank you for so much!

Solution Tree Press would like to thank the following reviewers:

Kara Blakey
English Teacher
Kinard Middle School
Fort Collins, Colorado

Kris Krautkremer
Science Teacher
Dobyns-Bennett High School
Kingsport, Tennessee

Jessica Magelky
Language Arts Teacher
Kadoka Area High School
Kadoka, South Dakota

Tara Smith
Language Arts Teacher
Storm Grove Middle School
Vero Beach, Florida

Hollye Wright
English Teacher
Fern Creek High School
Louisville, Kentucky

Visit go.SolutionTree.com/instruction to download
the free reproducibles in this book.

Table of Contents

About the Author

 **Peg Grafwallner, MEd,** is an instructional coach and reading specialist at Ronald Reagan High School, an urban International Baccalaureate school located on the south side of Milwaukee, Wisconsin. Peg has more than twenty-five years of experience in the field of education. She began her career as an English teacher at a private high school and eventually became an alternative education teacher in a suburban district. She has taught graduate-level courses on reading and writing in the content areas, with an emphasis on differentiation and interventions. She now supports teachers in seamlessly embedding literacy without disrupting their classroom objectives. Peg models how to create comprehensive literacy lessons that enhance skill-building and coaches and assists teachers in creating these lessons.

Peg is a member of the Wisconsin State Reading Association (WSRA), the Wisconsin Council of Teachers of English (WCTE), the National Council of Teachers of English (NCTE), and the Association for Supervision and Curriculum Development (ASCD). As the parent of a gifted and talented son and a special education daughter, Peg offers a unique educational lens that focuses on supporting students of all abilities in realizing their potential in the classroom and beyond. She is a blogger, author, and national presenter whose topics include coaching, engagement, and inclusion. Her articles have appeared in *The Missouri Reader*, the *Exceptional Parent*, the *WSRA Journal*, and the *Illinois Reading Council Journal*. She has written for several websites and blogs, including Edutopia, *ASCD InService*, Education Week's *Classroom Q&A*

With Larry Ferlazzo, KQED's *In the Classroom*, and *Literacy & NCTE*. She has also appeared on numerous podcasts such as *Cult of Pedagogy, BAM! Radio*, and *Ed: Conversations About the Teaching Life*. Peg is also the author of *Lessons Learned From the Special Education Classroom: Creating Opportunities for All Students to Listen, Learn, and Lead*.

Peg received a bachelor's degree in English and a mentoring certification from Cardinal Stritch University, a master's degree in curriculum and instruction and an alternative education certification from Marian College, and a reading specialist certification from the University of Wisconsin–Milwaukee.

To learn more about Peg's work, visit www.peggrafwallner.com and follow her on Twitter @PegGrafwallner.

To book Peg Grafwallner for professional development, contact pd@SolutionTree.com.

Introduction

Most K–12 novice and veteran teachers emphasize their course content but struggle to deliver it in engaging and inspiring ways. While sharing content is indeed important, it is equally important that teachers design a classroom structure that creates enthusiasm and excitement for learning. If teachers do not form a curious community of learners, the most crucial content will go unheard and unlearned. When teachers do not deliver content meaningfully, students get bored, tired, and frustrated. According to a 2010 German study, "Boredom 'instigates a desire to escape from the situation' that causes boredom" (Jason, 2017). Therefore, as students become increasingly bored, they look for ways to leave the classroom—the bathroom break, the trip to the nurse's office, the phone call home, or even daydreaming—anything to escape.

While observing, listening, and learning with teachers in classrooms, workshops, and graduate classes, I have noticed an emphasis on the immediate delivery of content but not necessarily a structured method with which to deliver it, implement it, or assess it such that it holds students' interest. Having such a structured method benefits both novice and veteran teachers because students will thrive knowing what the upcoming lesson will be about, how the teacher will implement that lesson, and how it will be assessed. For example, if a ninth-grade English lesson is focused on writing an academic essay, and the teacher introduces it in just those words, "Good morning students, today we will write an academic essay," students might be unclear, overwhelmed, and anxious. They might have questions, like the following: What *is* an academic essay? How do I write one? What background do I need to know?

How will I know if I've written a good one? Such questions can form a barrier to engagement when students aren't confident in receiving answers. Before the content is even delivered to students, teachers can engage students to want to be a part of the learning process by establishing a structure in which students know they will receive a clear road map with an opportunity to ask questions about the directions, a chance to see a model of the finished work, and the opportunity to reflect on the process.

Designing an organized, engaging, and motivating classroom experience does not have to be overwhelming or worrisome. In this book, I present the FRAME model, which is an easy-to-follow protocol that will help teachers support all students of all abilities. FRAME is a helpful acronym that includes five components: (1) *focus*, (2) *reach*, (3) *ask*, (4) *model*, and (5) *encourage*. This protocol for teachers and students clarifies learning expectations and provides a consistent structure of support. FRAME eliminates wasted time and helps the teacher stay true to the lesson while students move systematically through the learning. By eliminating the element of surprise, teachers can set up students to feel enthusiastic, excited, and curious. In short, they will be ready to learn.

Teachers can apply FRAME in three distinct ways. First, they can utilize it within the first ten minutes of class; FRAME offers teachers and their students a comprehensible opener that ensures all students understand what is being asked of them during the lesson. Second, during the lesson, applying each component of FRAME offers students the opportunity to solidify their understanding of learning expectations and demonstrate what they are expected to know and be able to do. In essence, FRAME offers teachers a highly adaptable framework to structure learning for students that lets them develop understanding of learning goals and demonstrate that learning in real and relevant ways. Third, teachers can use FRAME to improve the efficacy of their own classroom instruction through peer observations and feedback. To facilitate this third process, the tool "FRAME Peer Observation and Feedback Form for Teachers" (pages 105–107) offers teachers a valuable resource to collaborate with each other on their journey toward implementing FRAME with their classroom instruction.

Over the rest of this introduction, I will introduce you to the individual components of FRAME, the audience I've designed it for, details about its creation, and a primer for what you can expect from the rest of this book.

The Components of FRAME

The following text briefly explains each component of the FRAME model; upcoming chapters will investigate these components based on the three specific usage scenarios I just outlined.

Focus

If you want optimal learning to take place, it's vital that you focus your class on the goals for a day's lesson. A focused and structured classroom, one that is prepared for learning, helps students take the guesswork out of what comes next. Derrick Meador (2018) explains, "A structured classroom often translates to a safe classroom, one where students can enjoy themselves and focus on learning. In a structured learning environment, students are more likely to thrive and experience personal and academic growth." Using the FRAME model, the teacher establishes this focus by creating a learning intention and success criteria for each lesson that are student friendly and student centered; these help focus students of all abilities and all grade levels on their own progress and development.

Reach

Reach gives each student the personal attention that is so important in developing a sense of classroom community. Educator Janice Wyatt-Ross (2018) clarifies, "School leaders and classroom teachers should view their school or classroom spaces as culturally inclusive classroom communities where everyone is welcome." Acknowledging each student's presence with an engaging smile, individual eye contact, and his or her preferred name (pronounced correctly) supports a student's sense of self within the community. When you reach out to them, your students will be energetic community members and know that you will meet their ideas, critiques, successes, and challenges with respect, empathy, and mindfulness as they learn to determine and become their best selves.

Ask

It's no wonder teachers get discouraged when students don't seamlessly move through a lesson; often, this occurs because students have no idea where the learning is going, a frustrating experience for both teacher and student. Students will succeed at staying true to the learning intention and the success criteria only if they understand what you are asking them to know and be able to do. Therefore, it is important to teach students how to ask questions and analyze the expectations for the work they will soon undertake. If students do not understand the work ahead, as Connie M. Moss, Susan M. Brookhart, and Beverly A. Long (2011) write, "The teacher will always be the only one providing the direction, focusing on getting students to meet the instructional objectives." Teachers need to demonstrate how to ask robust questions and how to analyze the *what* of the learning intention and success criteria through a series of clarifying and probing questions. These clarifying and probing questions help students paraphrase the learning intention and success criteria, illustrating how to dive deep into the tasks ahead and why those tasks are valuable.

Model

When teachers model and provide instruction on the task, students are no longer unsure of what the finished product should include or how to arrive at it. When directions overwhelm students, or they get lost in the myriad steps to get their work done, they may become frustrated and check out. By modeling the process, the teacher takes the mystery and frustration out of students' work. Additionally, Marlynn K. Clayton (2010) expresses that a teacher breaking down a task "sends the message that you value the process of learning, not just the products." During this component, the teacher might show two or three pieces of the task along with the final product so that students visualize what the task is all about. For example, if the finished product is a data table showing the effects of climate change on water resources, an eleventh-grade environmental science teacher might begin with a list of how to shrink one's carbon footprint; then, he might offer two or three scholarly websites as a way for students to gather information; and finally, he might show an example of what a completed data table looks like. Modeling is meant as a brief overview of the upcoming work (not a detailed demonstration) to help students visualize both the finished product and the steps necessary to get there so they see that they, too, can accomplish the learning intention. As literacy specialist Rebecca Alber (2014) suggests, showing the finished product first "can guide students through each step of the process with the model of the finished product in hand."

Encourage

Finally, encourage students' work by praising the process of that work in a supportive classroom community. *Praising the process* means that you encourage students' hard work, strategies, and perseverance, rather than just praising intelligence (Stanford Alumni, 2014). By praising the process, you are offering your students vital feedback about the work; not about the student. Annie Brock and Heather Hundley

(2018) contend that "process praise…acknowledges effort, strategies, or actions that contributed to the success of the task" (p. 74).

You have designed a lesson that will support your students' curiosity; therefore, tell them the work might challenge and, at times, perplex them. But remind them they have support within the classroom community to understand the learning intention and conquer the success criteria because the teacher has taken specific steps to create a safe community. Teachers can drive the presence of this support home for students by reaching out to each of them, encouraging them to ask about their learning, modeling the process of the learning, and giving them the chance to reflect on *how* they learned. These processes create a caring and respectful classroom of learners.

The Audience for FRAME

Teachers can use FRAME in all grade levels, in all content areas, and with students of all abilities. This is because the model itself is designed for flexibility. You can adapt FRAME for all your students' academic, personal, and emotional needs, such that *all* students have the chance to succeed based on their own differing abilities. Developing learners will appreciate the consistency that FRAME offers and will be able to use those first ten minutes of structured classroom time to organize and prepare for learning. The routine and structure that FRAME provides give intention and significance to your lesson plans.

As with students, FRAME is meant for *all* educators. Novice teachers will appreciate the explicit and systematic method of introducing structure during the first ten minutes of class. According to Kitty Green (2006):

> Without such a structure, fledgling teachers hope for the best, frequently viewing results as either total success or complete failure. In reality, neither emotion supports the development of a new teacher into a more reflective practitioner—the central practice of a professional educator. (p. 1)

When they apply FRAME, novice teachers do not have to hope for the best. Instead, intentionally and deliberately implementing the structured FRAME approach is designed to make them more reflective practitioners and more professional educators.

Veteran teachers may feel that they already know some of the content in this book. However, according to Brown University assistant professor of education and economics John P. Papay, "Teacher quality is not something that's fixed. It does develop, and if you're making a decision about a teacher's career, you should be looking at that dynamic" (as cited in Sawchuk, 2015). Teachers must continue to hone their teaching practice to stay vital in the classroom. Therefore, what makes this book different is how it compiles these familiar practices into one approach that provides students with a context for learning. The FRAME model has many common practices within it, but evidence and examples throughout the book illustrate FRAME's unique perspective on implementation and reflection.

FRAME's benefits also go beyond the classroom because it helps build the kind of teacher efficacy that is crucial if schools want to retain exemplary teachers and offer the best learning experiences to students. By creating an *everyone-can-improve* motto, teachers know that they are a work in progress and that they can continue to hone their craft as they move forward on their educational journey. Terry Bramschreiber (2012) writes, "When teachers observe and learn from one another, better teaching practices, more student learning, and more positive evaluations result." Therefore, applying FRAME to peer observation and feedback among teachers is a natural next step. Using FRAME for teachers' peer observation and feedback gives them the opportunity to utilize guiding questions as a means to gather anecdotal data from peer observations and reflect on those data. In addition, the guiding questions encourage conversation between or among teachers that might not otherwise take place. Creating space and time for peer observation and feedback among teachers allows them to reflect on and hone their practice, build teacher efficacy and teacher empowerment, and make specific changes as necessary, all within a risk-free, nonjudgmental, teacher-driven environment.

Finally, FRAME gives administrators the opportunity to help teachers who may need extra support. Because FRAME is a specific approach meant for all content areas and all grade levels, the developing teacher can follow the structured protocol to gain effective strategies. According to the Inclusive Schools Network (2015), principals' responsibilities include "ensuring educational strategies are in place that support effective learning for all students. They serve as a facilitator, guide and supporter of quality instructional practices." Therefore, as facilitators and guides, principals can offer the FRAME protocol to ensure strategies that empower the developing teacher and help establish an exemplary classroom experience for students.

The Creation of FRAME

FRAME's foundations started in the classroom. As an instructional coach and reading specialist for my school, I am often asked to observe student teachers in various departments so I can offer feedback and recommend literacy strategies that will enhance their lessons. A biology teacher in my school once asked if I would observe her student teacher. The student teacher taught three class periods of tenth-grade biology. On this particular day, students were presenting on a topic of their choice. They were able to choose from reproduction and cell division, heredity and genetics, evolution, and ecology. The classroom teacher felt another set of eyes would benefit the novice teacher.

On a Monday morning, I walked into the biology classroom about ten minutes before the bell, ready to observe the student teacher preparing students for the first day of presentations. I expected to see her in the hall greeting students. However, she had not yet arrived. Her door was open, and students were milling about, but she was not there. About five minutes before class started, she walked in, went straight to her computer, logged in, and told students that they should get in their groups and get ready to present. She took off her coat, grabbed her clipboard, and motioned for the first group to stand in front of the class.

She called this first group to begin presenting. The group members appeared unsure and nervous, stumbling through their presentation. I wondered if they could have benefited from a structured introduction to the class—an organized beginning meant to prepare them for the learning ahead. I later learned that student groups had been given three days of in-class time to work on their presentation, including conducting research into the topic and creating a visual for their presentation. However, even though students had been given the directions and had class time, they still seemed apprehensive.

After each group presented, the student teacher listed a series of things the students *should* have done (for example, "You needed to speak louder" or "Your slide was difficult to read" or "Did you proofread your slideshow?"). Because she directed most comments toward presentation techniques instead of content, I wondered what the goal of these presentations was. What were students supposed to know and be able to do?

At the end of the presentations, she read a list of the students who were presenting the next day. After that, the bell rang, and the class was over.

During the class, I took specific observational notes that I would share with the student teacher to help her modify the classroom culture and gather explicit feedback from her forthcoming student groups. When I reflected on the class and my notes, I realized that students had missed out on a culture of learning, a structured method to begin class that would have supported their understanding of the work they were doing. Students had missed the *why* and the *how*—the relevance—of their vital work.

Similarly, this student teacher knew her content and was excited to have students share what they had read and researched with their peers. However, she missed the valuable opportunity to connect with the students. As I looked around the room, I noticed there were no learning intention and success criteria posted for students to observe. These should be written *the day before* and posted where students can see them throughout the lesson. If the teacher is busy writing the learning intention and success criteria as students walk in the door, students may see them as trivial.

Consider this from the students' perspective. Although it was obvious they would be presenting that morning, what was the point of the presentations? Why did they create them? Why was it necessary to share the information with their peers? Without a learning intention and success criteria, these questions were not asked, discussed, or answered. In addition, due to time, the student teacher couldn't share a personal greeting with them and detect, perhaps, their anxiety about the presentation. If she had, she could have suggested some mindful breathing techniques as students took their seats. Once students had taken their seats, she could have begun what would become the ten-minute FRAME protocol—asking students to read and paraphrase the learning intention and success criteria to determine their understanding of the task; modeling briefly the process of an exemplary presentation, such as what makes a captivating beginning, a riveting middle, and a compelling ending; and acknowledging the difficulty of the research work or recognizing the trepidation students might feel about presenting to their peers. Because this protocol was not put in place, students were uncertain about the ultimate goal of their presentation and why it mattered. I was excited to collaborate with this student teacher to help her realize the value of that connection.

I went to the second day of student presentations to determine if what I had witnessed the day before was an anomaly or standard procedure. Unfortunately, the pattern repeated itself. I met with the student teacher after that second class and shared some of my observations and ideas with her. I hoped to help her reframe the remaining set of student presentations. Using my notes, I explained what I had seen and offered the following suggestions.

- Since she had stated no learning intention or success criteria, we could work together to write an explicit learning intention and success criteria for the remaining presentations.

- If time was an issue for her in the morning, perhaps she could walk around to student groups as they were getting organized and say hello or give students a conversation question, such as, "What movie best describes you?" that could begin building a classroom community.

- I offered to demonstrate how she could call on two or three students and ask them to paraphrase the learning intention and success criteria for greater student understanding, thereby helping students unpack the *what* of the work they were doing.

- I offered to help create a minipresentation she could show to the students. Viewing a finished presentation, maybe even two or three slides, might help alleviate anxiety and support students in the *how* of the learning.

- I presented the idea of creating a list of encouraging phrases she could use that focused on process, and not necessarily product, as students completed their presentations. Such phrases could include, "That particular example makes me want to learn more," "Explain why you chose that example to include in your slide," and, "This is interesting information. What do you want your audience to gain from that information?"

The student teacher listened but seemed overwhelmed. I realized that it was simply too ambitious to implement all these suggestions before the next set of presentations. I asked her what she thought we could reasonably implement before the next class. She decided we could write a learning intention and success criteria, and she could greet students at the beginning of class.

We met again before the next class and created a learning intention and success criteria together. During our meeting, I learned the student teacher had jotted down some ideas of what she wanted her students to learn but didn't share them with her class. In researching, planning, implementing, and reflecting on the student presentations, she had forgotten about the learning intention and success criteria. Understanding this was also a learning experience for her, I explained that many things could get lost in the shuffle as we try to design the best, most engaging classroom lesson we can. I explained that using a framework for those first few minutes of class might help keep her and her students on track. Once we developed the learning intention and success criteria, we wrote them down on butcher paper and hung them in the front of the classroom so students could see them as they walked into class. During the next class, as students were preparing for presentations and getting organized for the learning, she walked around the room, greeted each group at its table, and offered positive words to those who had not yet presented.

Once students were ready, the student teacher read the learning intention and success criteria aloud. Unfortunately, she did not have enough time to unpack the why and how of the learning intention and success criteria because presentations were on a tight schedule. But she greeted her students specifically, and we accomplished a learning intention and success criteria where they had not existed before. At the end of the presentations, the student teacher and I met one more time. She said she had implemented two specific components in her other classes: (1) writing the next day's learning intention and success criteria at the end of the day and hanging it in a specific spot so students could see it, and (2) standing outside the classroom door and interacting with each student before the bell rang. In taking just these two steps, she noticed specific improvement. She shared that students seemed more relaxed and less anxious about their presentations once she started providing structure at the beginning of class. As a result of the structure, she thought students appeared to have a more confident demeanor. She was also learning things about her students she had never known before. She told me, "Several of my students walked in the Dreamers March. I didn't know that," and she appreciated them sharing their lives with her.

She explained that she had never really thought much about the beginning of class and instead was more content oriented. But after our discussions, she wanted to continue working with me on ways to structure those first ten minutes for optimal student success.

It was through this process that I created the concept of FRAME and its components that make up those first ten minutes of class: focus, reach, ask, model, and encourage. Over time, I observed how the components of FRAME appeared within a typical classroom lesson; so from there, I applied FRAME to the entire classroom experience.

FRAME was born out of a need to help a fellow teacher. The teacher had completed her lesson; there was no doubt she knew her content and wanted her students to know it too. However, without properly organizing her students' thinking, the lesson fell short. My collaboration with the student teacher helped me realize the value of using FRAME during the first ten minutes, during the lesson, and as a check for understanding. I designed FRAME as a resource for teachers to implement some research-based ideas, along with practical classroom strategies. Focusing on an instructional target, reaching students to intentionally build community in the classroom, asking questions and analyzing expectations to demonstrate achievement, modeling desired outcomes, and encouraging students will develop a community of curious learners ready to engage with the content and understand why it is valuable.

How to Use This Book

Teachers are eager to implement the content they have learned or the lesson they have designed. They are excited to support students and help them become better readers, writers, mathematicians, historians, artists, and knowledgeable citizens. However, they sometimes forget that as valuable as their content is, the lesson will have little impact if their students aren't prepared and poised for learning. If students aren't ready to learn, the best lesson will fail.

Author Pernille Ripp (2015) explains that students want to know the greater purpose behind the tasks they must accomplish, and she details how she helped students know the purpose of the lesson by spending time deconstructing standards and speaking about the connections between things. Educators and program and policy experts Peter Goss and Julie Sonnemann (2017) further find, "When students are engaged in class, they learn more. It is vital that teachers create the right classroom climate for learning: raising student expectations, developing a rapport with students; establishing routines; challenging students to participate and take risks" (p. 3).

Unfortunately, many teachers, even experienced teachers, dive right into the material without implementing a structure or routine in their class. Students want to know the big picture; they want to know where they're going and how to get there. If the class has no structure, students are apt to become disengaged and disinterested. FRAME aims to eliminate the trepidation that students might feel upon entering the classroom and, instead, provide a basis for community building and learning and help teachers get their students ready for the important job of learning. The goal of this book is to help teachers systematically launch the first ten minutes of class and continue applying that structure throughout the lesson.

In addition, teachers have the option to apply all or individual components of FRAME. Teachers can determine if students need more or less time on specific components, thereby giving teachers flexibility and explicit control over all elements of their classroom.

Chapter 1 contains foundational information about learning intentions and success criteria and how to write them. Chapter 2 describes how to apply FRAME within the first ten minutes of class. Chapter 3 offers ideas for how to apply FRAME throughout a lesson or instructional unit. With the FRAME structure and process established, we turn to how you can establish and grow FRAME's adoption in your school. To that end, chapter 4 offers suggestions on how to prepare for and conduct teacher observations utilizing FRAME; observations give both teacher and observer the opportunity to share strategies and resources that support classroom instruction and align expectations for students' learning.

Each chapter features two exciting recurring elements: the Exemplary Classroom applies the chapter's topic to an authentic classroom experience, and the Do-Now Suggestions for Your Classroom or Collaborative Team that end each chapter give educators a list of pedagogical questions to spark reflection and schoolwide or districtwide conversation and perhaps opportunities for growth and change.

The appendix includes a blank template for following the FRAME structure, along with sample completed templates for elementary school, middle school, and high school lessons that give teachers concrete examples of what FRAME could look like in their classroom. It also provides a reproducible copy of the "FRAME Peer Observation and Feedback Form for Teachers" tool I introduce in chapter 4. These examples are meant to present ideas and suggestions for adding FRAME to your tools of best practice and solid pedagogical standards.

Conclusion

FRAME offers a structured guide to daily teacher preparation and planning that also builds a firm foundation for student readiness. The components of FRAME are grounded in research-based methods and practical strategies meant for students of all abilities and for all grade levels. In addition, the FRAME protocol is flexible; teachers can determine which components their students most need to achieve success and accordingly spend more or less time on each component. This book will give teachers what they need to understand FRAME and implement it in their classroom.

Now, it's time to get your FRAME on!

CHAPTER 1

How to Create Learning Intentions and Success Criteria

Classroom teachers need to know how to create engaging, exciting, and enthusiastic opportunities for learning, no matter the content area. But in many teacher-preparation programs, teacher candidates spend the majority of their time concentrating on content-specific pedagogies and content background (Martin & Mulvihill, 2017). Teacher-preparation programs tend to emphasize discipline-specific knowledge rather than comprehensive pedagogical expertise. While content-area expertise is undeniably important, as content knowledge is vital for creating positive outcomes on classroom assessments and national standardized tests, you must first focus your students for learning if you expect that content to be explicit and effective.

Designing a structured, engaging, and motivating classroom experience takes practice but does not have to be all-encompassing. Establishing the learning intention and success criteria students will focus on throughout a lesson or unit will help you apply structures and routines that support all students of all abilities. These pieces are the foundation of the lesson, so it is important that you always stay mindful of student learning as you write them. As an essential prelude to the FRAME-specific content in chapters 2–4, this chapter provides foundational information for writing each of these items, as well as important considerations to keep in mind.

Learning Intentions: What Do You Want Students to Understand?

Douglas Fisher and Nancy Frey (2018) define a *learning intention* as "what you want students to know and be able to do by the end of one or more lessons" (p. 82). Think of learning intentions as the building blocks of an overall unit. Crafting a quality learning intention takes planning. Often, teachers will use an activity as their learning intention, but a true learning intention goes beyond an activity. As an example, a learning intention applying an activity might read *Students can use think, pair, share to complete the mathematics worksheet*. In this particular example, *think, pair, share* is an activity. It is not the learning intention as it does not establish a skill to learn. Rather, the goal of this poorly constructed learning intention is the completion of the worksheet.

A valid and effective learning intention should focus on the goal of the learning—the thing you want your students to know and do. For example, a well-written learning intention for middle school mathematics might read *I can use proportional relationships to solve problems*. The teacher might still recommend using think, pair, share so students can work together to solve the problems, or the teacher might distribute a worksheet so students can practice proportional relationships, but the goal of this learning intention is to have students *using* proportional relationships to solve problems. By using proportional relationships, students are also applying, practicing, and proving what they know and what they are able to do.

When teachers come back from an engaging conference or inspirational workshop, they frequently want to use all they learned to help their students. But giving your students a brand-new graphic organizer or an exciting educational technology tool and asking them to complete it or explore it is also not a learning intention—these tools are merely vehicles meant to enhance the learning. What are students supposed to know and be able to *do* with the graphic organizer or the educational technology tool? If you are struggling to come up with an answer, you probably have not created a lesson with a clear learning intention.

In addition to establishing a skill to learn, learning intentions should engage and motivate students by giving them one or more questions they want to solve. These questions are more likely to engage students in introspection if they are real, relevant, and relatable to the student. For example, if you are simply asking students to locate the main idea of a text or define a vocabulary word without providing them with context relevant to them, you can assume students will quickly lose interest. Learning intentions are meant to guide student learning. According to Fisher and Frey (2018), "Without a clear learning destination in mind, lessons wander, and students become confused and frustrated" (p. 82). This is why creating an interesting learning intention will help students stay focused and involved in the lesson. In addition, the focus of the day's lesson should be manageable, or else students may become anxious if they feel they cannot meet the learning intention. "Even the 'best' lesson is worthless if students aren't engaged, or don't believe they will be able to complete the work" (Rollins, 2015).

As you review your notes for the next day's lesson, consider what you want your students to know and do with the information you will share. This gets at the heart of the learning intention. It is important to create the learning intention first, then determine the success criteria needed to meet the learning intention, and then create a series of open-ended questions that help engage students in cognitive thinking and empower them to take classroom risks. As educator Paula Denton (2007) writes, "Instead of predictable answers, open-ended questions elicit fresh and sometimes even startling insights and ideas, opening minds and enabling teachers and students to build knowledge together."

Following are some examples of high-quality learning intentions, loosely derived from the Common Core State Standards (National Governors Association Center for Best Practices [NGA] & Council of Chief State School Officers [CCSSO], 2010a, 2010b), in a variety of content areas and grade levels. Note that the Common Core State Standards are merely a starting point, an inspiration for learning depending upon what the student needs. I have reworded them to create a series of student-friendly *I can* statements.

- **Second-grade mathematics:** I can understand the place value of numbers up to 1,000.

- **Third-grade reading:** I can find and tell the main idea of the texts read in class and share examples with my peers.

- **Sixth- to eighth-grade science and technical subjects:** I can learn the differences among superstition, pseudoscience, and science.

- **Eighth-grade U.S. history:** I can discuss, explain, and research the events leading to the American Revolution and their influence on the formation of the Constitution.

- **Ninth- and tenth-grade English language arts (ELA):** I can understand the role and proper use of figurative language in a narrative.

- **Eleventh- and twelfth-grade writing:** I can write an argument to support a claim using valid reasoning and relevant and sufficient evidence.

Simply telling students the official standard they need to learn is not nearly enough. Students must be able to grasp the task they are to do and feel that they can do it. Additionally, teachers need the freedom to adapt such standards for the students in front of them. This might involve extending a standard to advance learning further or even dial it back if students are struggling. If the learning intention is not written in a developmentally appropriate way, students will not understand what they are supposed to know and be able to do, and when that happens, engagement will suffer (Moss et al., 2011).

These learning intentions are exemplary because they go beyond basic activities and lead to explanation, discussion, application, and reflection. For example, in the eighth-grade history example, students will focus on the events leading to the American Revolution by discussing, explaining, and researching the influence of the formation of the U.S. Constitution. This learning intention inspires students to use what they have read and researched to engage in interesting discussions.

Conversely, an insufficient learning intention for this topic might read *I will study the events leading to the American Revolution and how it led to the formation of the U.S. Constitution.* Unfortunately, this learning intention doesn't clarify how the American Revolution led to the formation of the Constitution. Just studying the events doesn't give students a clear road map on what they are going to know and be able to do. The word *study* is ambiguous and doesn't offer any examples to students on how they are going to learn about the formation of the Constitution.

Similarly, in the ninth- and tenth-grade ELA example, just locating or talking about figurative language is hardly noteworthy, but understanding how figurative language can intensify a narrative encourages students to have a dialogue and defend their examples with stimulating textual evidence.

Crafting a dynamic learning intention requires having success criteria that will support all students toward reaching the learning intention's goal; therefore, determining those steps is vital to student comprehension.

Success Criteria: How Can Students Show They Know and Understand?

If a learning intention is the destination, then success criteria are the milestones necessary to reach the destination. Fisher and Frey (2018) define *success criteria* as "a means for teachers and students to utilize feedback specifically oriented to the learning intentions. They clarify how a task or assignment will be judged" (p. 83). This judgment illustrates to students what they specifically need to do to accomplish the learning intention.

When determining your success criteria, consider the goal of your learning intention and how your students will, via the milestones you have determined, demonstrate, apply, prove, or synthesize what they have learned to meet that goal. Your students want to share their hard work—give them every opportunity to do so. Teachers should identify the success criteria based on the learning intention and scaffold the success criteria using a series of learning progressions to help students reach a specific milestone (success criterion).

Identifying the Success Criteria

After the teacher has created the learning intention, the next step is to write a series of success criteria based on that intention. There is no recipe for success in identifying these criteria; rather, teachers must ask themselves, "What milestones must the student reach to meet the learning intention?" This is a process that improves with practice, but I will show you multiple examples in this section to help you think about how you would craft your own success criteria.

According to the National Council for Curriculum and Assessment (2015), "Success criteria are linked to learning intentions. They are developed by the teacher and/or the student and describe what the success looks like" (p. 5). As an example, if I want my third-grade students to learn to write an opinion paragraph, using reasons to support their point of view, my learning intention would look like the following.

- **Learning intention:** I can write an opinion paragraph that lists three reasons for my opinion.

- **Success criteria:** I know I am successful because—

    1. I can brainstorm ideas about a topic in which I have a strong opinion

    2. I can list reasons about the topic

3. I can explain why the reasons are important

4. I can write an opinion paragraph sharing my three reasons

There is no ideal number of success criteria to use, and the number of success criteria necessary to meet a learning intention is as variable as the possibilities for learning intentions themselves. After constructing the learning intention, the teacher needs to decide the necessary steps to achieve that goal. Some learning intentions may only need three or four criteria for students to meet them successfully. Others could require more. If a teacher can only come up with one or two success criteria, or if the number of them becomes unwieldy (for example, ten or more), that indicates a need to, respectively, broaden the scope of a learning intention to encompass more learning or break it up into multiple learning intentions to avoid overwhelming students. What is important is that the success criteria a teacher determines are numbered to show the progression needed to achieve the learning intention.

Using the same grade-specific learning intentions previously offered as examples in the Learning Intentions section (page 14), let's look at some more examples of scaffolded success criteria.

- **Second-grade mathematics:**

  - *Learning intention*—I can understand the place value of numbers up to 1,000.

  - *Success criteria*—I know I am successful because . . .

    1. I can explain the place value of digits in a number

    2. I can read, write, and order numbers and explain my understanding of them

    3. I can identify numbers before and after one thousand

    4. I can expand and name numbers up to three digits

- **Third-grade reading:**

  - *Learning intention*—I can find and tell the main idea of the texts read in class and share examples with my peers.

  - *Success criteria*—I know I am successful because . . .

    1. I can ask questions about the text

    2. I can answer questions about the text

    3. I can use my questions and answers about the text to find the main idea

- **Sixth- to eighth-grade science and technical subjects:**

  - *Learning intention*—I can learn the differences among superstition, pseudoscience, and science.

  - *Success criteria*—I know I am successful because . . .

    1. I can define *superstition*, *pseudoscience*, and *science*

    2. I can demonstrate the differences using a graphic organizer

    3. I can find real-life examples of superstition, pseudoscience, and science and share them with the class

- **Eighth-grade U.S. history:**

  - *Learning intention*—I can discuss, explain, and research the events leading to the American Revolution and their influence on the formation of the Constitution.

  - *Success criteria*—I know I am successful because . . .

    1. I can create a timeline of the events leading to the American Revolution

    2. I can explain the impact of these events to a partner

    3. I can show the connection among these important events and how they helped create the Constitution

- **Ninth- and tenth-grade English language arts:**

  - *Learning intention*—I can understand the role and proper use of figurative language in a narrative.

  - *Success criteria*—I know I am successful because . . .

    1. I can identify imagery and symbolism in a passage from *Jane Eyre* (Brontë, 1997)

    2. I can explain the impact that the use of imagery and symbolism has on the reader, using evidence from *Jane Eyre* to explain my reasoning

    3. I can write a personal narrative using effective imagery and create a compelling symbol

- **Eleventh- and twelfth-grade writing:**

  - *Learning intention*—I can write an argument to support a claim using valid reasoning and relevant and sufficient evidence.

- *Success criteria*—I know I am successful because . . .

  1. I can brainstorm a variety of arguments to support my claim

  2. I can locate key words and phrases to determine bias or prejudice in the various arguments I have created

  3. I can point out the strengths and limitations of my arguments based on research

  4. I can distinguish by language and research which argument is based on valid, relevant, and sufficient evidence

Writing a learning intention with success criteria that are interesting and engaging takes time, practice, and possibly a collaborative effort with both other teachers and students. In fact, your students can be your best gauge in determining if your success criteria are effective. As a group, do they show enthusiasm? Are they confused or lost? Are they bored?

According to Michael McDowell (2018), "Often . . . success criteria [is] one set list for students to meet." He goes on to say, "More often than not, students are unfamiliar with the material to be learned and are therefore unable to decipher the right sequence of success criteria to be met over time." Therefore, the success criteria reflect a progression of skills that demonstrate complexity. When the student has mastered the first success criterion, that student moves on to the next one.

In addition, while the success criteria for each learning intention apply to all student abilities, they provide a means for teachers to identify which students are struggling or excelling and for students to self-assess their own gaps in understanding or their success (Freibrun, 2019). This helps teachers differentiate instruction accordingly. Note that this is not just about checking off boxes, but a means to motivate students. Marine Freibrun (2019) cites Douglas Fisher, Nancy Frey, Olivia Amador, and Joseph Assof (2019) on the value of success criteria on motivation: "Success criteria have been shown to increase students' internal motivation. It provides students with clear, specific, and attainable goals that spark motivation. Even in some of the most reluctant learners (p. 20)."

Once those gaps appear, the teacher and students can determine their next steps to help bridge that gap. Some of those next steps may include dedicated time for students to self-assess so they can "return periodically to particular rubrics to compare their work from earlier in the year to more recent efforts" (Fisher & Frey, 2018, p. 83), discussions among peers so learners can gather information about how their work compares to the work of their peers, or a conversation with the teacher to recognize the students' missing connections or lack of understanding toward a success criterion. Therefore, scaffolded success criteria support students' various ability levels, and valuable feedback conversations help students in their opportunity to self-assess and self-reflect.

Using Learning Progressions

When creating success criteria, teachers will find it worthwhile to apply *learning progressions* (Ainsworth & Viegut, 2015), the strategy of focusing on basic skills and then moving toward higher-order-thinking skills. According to Larry Ainsworth and Donald Viegut (2015), learning progressions are the building blocks of instruction that help students understand how to get to the goals of the larger units of study. Consider learning progressions the scaffolding techniques necessary to move from one step to another.

As an example, if the larger unit of study in a ninth-grade ELA class is learning how to analyze, then students need to know how to break down a text. Therefore, to achieve that goal of analysis, the learning intention would be *I can understand how to write an analytical essay*. However, before students can write an essay, they need to learn how to write a thesis paragraph. This becomes the first step in the success criteria. The learning progressions toward this step would be the three basic skills necessary to write a thesis paragraph: (1) students brainstorm possible thesis statements, (2) students practice writing thesis statements, and (3) students share their thesis statements with their peers for feedback and revision.

Each learning progression guides the student toward a success criterion, just as each success criterion guides the student toward the learning intention. The progressions also progressively activate higher-order-thinking skills in students. These particular English building blocks—brainstorming, writing practice, and feedback—can transfer to other content disciplines and easily transfer to real-world situations. In this example, each instructional building block is linked to the overall learning intention of students' achieving mastery in analyzing text.

As figure 1.1 (page 22) illustrates, success criteria help students see the learning progressions as they complete one step and move on to the next. This progression of skill demonstrates student knowledge and understanding. So if brainstorming thesis statements is the first building block of the success criteria, that basic skill is necessary to move toward the next skill.

In this particular example, the teacher scaffolds the steps necessary for students to learn how to write an analytical paper. The teacher builds in supports to enhance

Learning Intention: I can understand how to write an analytical essay.	
Success Criteria: I know I am successful because . . .	**Learning Progressions**
1. I can develop a thesis statement.	a. Brainstorm thesis statements. b. Practice writing a thesis statement. c. Get feedback from peers.
2. I can write and revise a body paragraph.	a. Create a topic sentence. b. Write three supporting pieces of evidence. c. Analyze each piece of evidence. d. Develop a closing sentence. e. Edit the paragraph by partaking in a structured peer review.
3. I can write a conclusion.	a. Create a transition. b. Restate the thesis statement. c. End with a strong global message.

Figure 1.1: Scaffolding success criteria—ELA example.

learning and aid in the mastery of each task. He or she does this by systematically building on students' experiences and knowledge as they are learning new skills.

Let's consider another example—a ninth-grade physical education unit of study called *lifetime sports*. In this unit, students will learn about a variety of sports that people can play all through their lives with few (if any) adverse physical effects. One of those sports is badminton. Therefore, the learning intention in physical education is *I can learn how to play badminton*. Students will need to learn the basic skills or success criteria needed to play the game. First, students would need to learn the terms associated with badminton and what they mean. Next, students would need to learn the rules of the game and how to apply them. Finally, the students would need to stand on a badminton court, get a feel for the racket, practice their serve and swing, and eventually play the game. All these steps are the basic skills needed to play badminton. Therefore, a teacher might write the success criteria as follows.

- **Success criteria:** I know I am successful because—

    1. I can define the terms of badminton

    2. I can define the rules of the game and apply them

    3. I can stand on a badminton court and practice my serve and my swing

These learning progressions are the building blocks that make up the game of badminton, while the overall unit of study is *lifetime sports*. In this particular example, each building block of instruction is linked to the overall learning intention of students' eventually achieving mastery in understanding how to play badminton (see figure 1.2).

Learning Intention: I can learn how to play badminton.	
Success Criteria: I know I am successful because . . .	**Learning Progressions**
1. I can define the terms of badminton.	a. Create flashcards using 3 × 5 note cards. Write the terms on one side and the definitions on the other. b. Practice the definitions with peers. c. Match the objects used in badminton to the corresponding note cards.
2. I can define the rules of the game and apply them.	a. Read the rules of the game. b. Watch a badminton game, and apply the rules. c. With a partner, study the rules of the game.
3. I can stand on a badminton court and practice my serve and my swing.	a. Practice holding the racket and swinging it. b. Play a full game of badminton with a partner. c. Observe other peers playing, and referee their game to practice knowledge of the rules.

Figure 1.2: Scaffolding success criteria—physical education example.

When writing success criteria, list all the learning progressions, or scaffolded steps, so students see the beginning and the end. By seeing the breakdown of the guiding steps for each set of learning progressions, students can also see that their learning is a process, and, by accomplishing one step at a time, they will eventually meet and master the learning intention.

Teachers can give sets of learning progressions to students as a suggestion handout or ask students to brainstorm what they think they will need to do for each success criterion. As an example, when discussing how to achieve the first success criterion in figure 1.2, *I can define the terms of badminton*, the teacher could ask the students how *they* think they could achieve that success criterion. Students could work in small groups to brainstorm some ideas and write them down in a notebook. Then, as they work toward the success criteria, students could check off the ideas they have done. Later on, this brief and informal checklist could be the foundation of a reflective conversation between the teacher and the students to determine the success of meeting the learning intention.

Considerations for Writing Learning Intentions and Success Criteria

When writing learning intentions and success criteria, teachers need to consider intentional language, quality, clarity, and student choice.

Intentional Language

The wording of learning intentions and success criteria has implications for student choice and empowerment. As you write your learning intention and success criteria statements, be intentional about the language you use. Beginning these statements with either *I can* or *I will* implies a sense of knowing and doing; however, *I can* statements are stronger because they convey confidence in a student's ability to be a learner. These statements tell students that they can meet the goal, but it is up to them to choose to do so. This gives students more ownership over their learning and requires more commitment and engagement from the student. On the other hand, *I will* is not as strong in its confidence and, in a way, implies, "I will learn this information . . . *someday*." *I will* also says to students that the teacher has prescribed an outcome for them, and they are obligated to meet it regardless of whether they do. I recommend *I can* statements for confidence and conviction.

Quality

The quality of the learning intention and success criteria is imperative to student understanding and student engagement. If students perceive a lesson will be busywork or lack relevance, they may choose not to participate or engage in it. When choosing a learning intention, keep it relevant and relatable. Students may not immediately see the relevance of the learning intention; it is up to you to show them its significance. As an example, if you want students to find the main idea in a text, they will likely ask you why: "Why is the main idea important? What is the purpose? Why should *I* care?" These questions are valid, and your answers are important to your teacher credibility. Taking the time to answer these questions demonstrates the importance of the learning intention and success criteria; but more important, it demonstrates that you value your students' learning. It shows you care about their learning and want to help them achieve. Use the following three questions to help determine if a learning intention is engaging and relevant for students.

1. **Does the learning intention link to a bigger picture that has purpose or relevance to the student?** As an example, if the learning intention for a tenth-grade environmental science class is *I can explain how microplastics get into my food supply*, students might find this learning intention interesting because it is purposeful and relevant to their own lives. They can gather information on how much microplastics *they* are eating and how that affects *their* growth.

2. **Do the verbs you use describe how a student will be inspired by engaging with a learning experience?** As Scott Davis (2014) writes in "Using Bloom's Taxonomy to Write Learning Outcomes," it's important to stay away from mundane verbs, such as "I can *study* the main idea of texts read in class," "I can *learn* about the American Revolution and the formation of the Constitution," or "I can *write* a paper." These verbs don't share a passion for learning but rather apathy toward knowledge. Davis (2014) suggests using and lists some active verbs from Benjamin S. Bloom's (1956) taxonomy that demonstrate "what a student will be able to do with the information or experience." When a student can personalize an experience—to do something with it—then the teacher knows his or her learning intention is effective.

3. **Did students find the learning intention interesting? Why or why not?** It is perfectly acceptable to ask students for direct feedback. Ask them what they want to study, and look for opportunities to connect that to your course curriculum. By gathering input from your students, you can learn their interests of study and as a result, write learning intentions specifically geared toward their interests.

Clarity

Instead of merely giving lip service to the learning intention and success criteria, it is imperative that you write a learning intention and success criteria in student-friendly language. Using teacher jargon to write the learning intention and success criteria baffles students, and students could view it as condescending or arrogant. Most state standards are written with the teacher in mind, not the student. For example, the

Common Core State Standards for second-grade English Language Arts 2.1 in reading informational text is, "Ask and answer such questions as *who, what, where, when, why,* and *how* to demonstrate understanding of key details in a text" (NGA & CCSSO, 2010a). While a typical second-grade student may not view this as condescending or arrogant because they might not yet know what those words mean, they would certainly be baffled by what they were supposed to do. Even for secondary students, such language does not provide the kind of relevance that would make a learning intention interesting. Therefore, student-friendly language always supports the learner and helps the learner know what he or she is supposed to know and be able to do.

Likewise, student-friendly learning intentions and success criteria also reduce tension, inspire a positive classroom community, and help students realize that this learning intention of success is meant for *them*—not for the teacher or for the principal observer. As educational researcher Barry J. Zimmerman states, "Students can't see, recognize, and understand what they need to learn until we translate the learning intention into developmentally appropriate, student-friendly, and culturally respectful language" (as cited in Hagler, 2017, p. 8).

Writing the learning intention and success criteria in student-friendly language helps students understand that their learning is important and that they will be able to achieve the expectations you have created for them.

Student Choice

Offering students choice based on their interests helps immerse them in the learning. For example, if fifth-grade students will be working with nonfiction text, learning about tornadoes, find a few well-written articles and write the learning intention and success criteria for each one. For students who are not yet reading independently, there are online websites, such as the Early Learning Academy at www.abcmouse.com, that provide resources for preK–3 students in mathematics, reading, science, art, and colors. Elementary websites such as ReadWorks (www.readworks.org), National Geographic Kids (https://kids.nationalgeographic.com), and Newsela (https://newsela.com) are appropriate resources for informational text. For middle school students, Science News for Students (www.sciencenewsforstudents.org), TweenTribune (www.tweentribune.com), and Newsela offer nonfiction resources. Finally, for high school students, Engage NY (www.engageny.org), Kelly Gallagher's Article of the Week (www.kellygallagher.org/article-of-the-week), and GoogleNews Archive (https://news.google.com/newspapers) are worthy nonfiction resources.

All these resources provide a variety of articles at various Lexile levels and in different interests. Note, however, the learning intention and success criteria should be similar across all articles to ensure that the lesson reflects the focused standard. Then allow students to choose the article that they find most interesting—one that covers a topic they want to learn more about—and they can share with their peers.

The following are examples of online resources adapted for multiple grade levels and likely to create a high level of student engagement because they represent relevant events and issues in the lives of students. The examples include resources, sample learning intentions, and success criteria a teacher could use with his or her class.

- **Global plastics pollution—high school example:** This resource on microplastics is something appropriate for high school students in an environmental science class or health class.

  - *Article*—"Microplastics Discovered in 'Extreme' Concentrations in the North Atlantic" (Damon & Laine, 2019; https://cnn.it /2P2M4rT)

  - *Learning intention*—I can evaluate the argument and specific claims made in the article, determining if the reasoning is valid and the evidence is relevant.

  - *Success criteria*—I know I am successful because . . .

    1. I can evaluate the argument and specific claims made in the article

    2. I can determine if the reasoning is valid (or not)

    3. I can assess if the evidence is relevant (or not)

    4. I can share my findings and counterarguments (if any) with my peers

- **Global plastics pollution—middle school example:** Here is the same topic—microplastics—using Newsela as a resource and applying a seventh-grade nonfiction learning intention and success criteria.

  - *Article*—"Small Particles of Plastic Have Found a Home in Arctic Snow, Scientists Say" (Associated Press, 2019; https://bit.ly /2KWC3Hy)

  - *Learning intention*—I can locate the five Ws (who, what, where, when, and why) of the article, and write a summary based on the five Ws.

- *Success criteria*—I know I am successful because . . .

    1. I can read and annotate the article

    2. I can pick out the five Ws (who, what, where, when, and why) of the article

    3. I can write a summary based on the five Ws

- **Global plastics pollution—elementary school example:** Here is the same topic—microplastics—using ReadWorks as a resource and applying a second-grade nonfiction learning intention and success criteria.

    - *Article*—"Take Care of Our Planet" (Weekly Reader, 2009; https://bit.ly/2w6DA9J)

    - *Learning intention*—I can pick out the who, what, where, when and why of the article and explain it to a peer.

    - *Success criteria*—I know I am successful because . . .

        1. I can read the article

        2. I can pick out the who, what, where, when, and why of the article

        3. I can explain the article to a peer

- **Gun violence and legislation—high school example:** This article on the #NeverAgain movement is an example of using a high school–level resource to engage students in current events in a history or social studies class.

    - *Article*—"What You Should Know About the March for Our Lives" (Andone, 2018; https://cnn.it/2Gj4iAL)

    - *Learning intention*—I can explain the significance of the March for Our Lives movement based on the article.

    - *Success criteria*—I know I am successful because . . .

        1. I can explain what the March for Our Lives movement is about, using the article as my reference

        2. I can underline the main points from the article and explain to my peers why those main ideas are significant

        3. I can actively listen to the feedback from my peers and, if warranted, revise my explanation

- **Gun violence and legislation—middle school example:** Using Science News for Students, here is the same topic—legislation to prevent gun violence—but applying a seventh-grade nonfiction learning intention and success criteria.

  - *Article*—"Strict Gun Laws Ended Mass Shootings in Australia" (Rosen, 2016; https://bit.ly/2TuKiy8)

  - *Learning intention*—I can give three examples of inferences from the text and explain why they are inferences.

  - *Success criteria*—I know I am successful because . . .

    1. I can read and annotate the article

    2. I can define the word *inference* and apply it

    3. I can find three inferences from the text and explain why they are inferences

- **Gun violence and legislation—elementary school example:** Here is the same topic—legislation to prevent gun violence—using Newsela as a resource and applying a third-grade nonfiction learning intention and success criteria.

  - *Article*—"Students Vote: Before the March, We Let Students Vote on Gun Laws" (Orens, 2018; https://bit.ly/2HkZNUP)

  - *Learning intention*—I can explain the main idea of the article, using details to explain how the students in the article support the main idea.

  - *Success criteria*—I know I am successful because . . .

    1. I can explain what the gun laws are about, using the article as my reference

    2. I can underline the main idea from the article and explain to my peers why that is the main idea

    3. I can locate details in the article and explain how they support the main idea

- **Race and peace and justice in society—high school example:** This article on the opening of the Legacy Museum and the National Memorial for Peace and Justice is an example of using a high school–level resource to engage students in a topic related to English language arts.

- *Article*—"A Lynching Memorial Is Opening" (Robertson, 2018; https://nyti.ms/2vK8yV0)

- *Learning intention*—I can develop awareness about the "A Lynching Memorial Is Opening" article and research information about the creation of the memorial.

- *Success criteria*—I know I am successful because . . .

  1. I can explain what the article is about to my peers

  2. I can research the background of the museum and its creation

  3. I can share that research with my peers and explain why this museum is important

- **Race and peace and justice in society—middle school example:** Here is the same topic—peace and justice in society—using TweenTribune as a resource and applying a seventh-grade nonfiction learning intention and success criteria.

  - *Article*—"U.S. Capitol's Statuary Hall to Get First State-Commissioned Statue of a Black American" (Fessenden, 2018; https://bit.ly/2yY7KdZ)

  - *Learning intention*—I can show the author's purpose in the article and analyze how the author separates her purpose from the purpose of other people.

  - *Success criteria*—I know I am successful because . . .

    1. I can read the article and show the author's purpose

    2. I can locate the author's purpose

    3. I can explain the author's purpose and how she separates her purpose from the purpose of other people

- **Race and peace and justice in society—elementary school example:** Here is the same topic—peace and justice in society—using ReadWorks as a resource and applying a fourth-grade nonfiction learning intention and success criteria.

  - *Article*—"American Government: Preamble to the United States Constitution" (ReadWorks, 2012; https://bit.ly/2Z6rwOW)

- *Learning intention*—I can explain concepts from a historical text, including what happened and why, based on specific information in the text.

- *Success criteria*—I know I am successful because . . .

    1. I can read and annotate the text

    2. I can explain three concepts from the text

    3. I can explain what happened in the text and why the three concepts are important

Upon reading these learning intentions, any student might stop and read them again because these topics all represent hot-button issues that often go ignored in school settings. Students understand that this work is important and timely because they hear about topics like immigration, school violence, and racism through different media sources and in discussions with family and friends. The ensuing discussion should encourage students to want to read the articles and discover the main idea on their own.

The Exemplary Classroom

Following a series of in-class observations and formative assessments, my colleague, Mrs. Abby Felten, and I realized students in her sophomore chemistry class would benefit from a vocabulary lesson focusing on numeral prefixes (such as *mono-*, *bi-*, *tri-*, *quad-*, and so on). Abby chose prefixes 1–5 since they are extremely common when naming covalent compounds and prefixes 6–10 because, while they are only occasionally used in chemistry, they are frequently used in day-to-day life.

Abby wanted students to utilize these prefixes to translate between formulas and names of covalent compounds. With practice, she wanted her students to be able to fluently switch between formula and name. Students in their sophomore year were also traditionally enrolled in geometry where they were also learning and utilizing this same vocabulary set; therefore, the learning intention did not focus just on Abby's class but also on the opportunity to transfer this information to other classes.

In designing her lesson, Abby created the following learning intention and supporting success criteria.

- **Learning intention:** I can effectively pronounce, define, and apply Greek prefixes for numbers 1–10 when reading something that is unfamiliar—in this class and in my other classes.

- **Success criteria:** I know I am successful because—

1. I can effectively pronounce Greek prefixes for numbers 1–10

2. I can effectively define Greek prefixes for numbers 1–10

3. I can effectively apply Greek prefixes for numbers 1–10

By scaffolding each component of the success criteria, students could self-assess where they had achieved mastery or where they needed more support.

To determine their understanding, students drew posters that showed a common object connected to a Greek prefix with the dictionary pronunciation written on the poster. As an example, one poster depicted a stop sign with the Greek prefix *Hexa* and the dictionary pronunciation written next to it. Another poster showed a hand with the Greek prefix *Penta* and the dictionary pronunciation written inside the hand. Through this exercise, students had an opportunity to align their understanding of the learning intention in a way that made sense to them, and they engaged because the learning intention was real, relevant, and relatable.

Conclusion

Writing a learning intention and success criteria that meet the needs of your students may seem daunting and, at times, overwhelming. However, without a purposeful learning intention and success criteria written in clear, student-friendly language, your lesson will fall flat. A well-crafted learning intention and success criteria are essential for implementing FRAME; they will guide the rest of your teaching, and ultimately, what your students should know and be able to do. By applying the suggestions in this chapter, such as using clear learning progressions, intentional language, clarity, and student choice, you will design a classroom community whose foundation is based on high teacher expectations and the development of empowered and confident students.

Do-Now Suggestions for Your Classroom or Collaborative Team

Reflect on the following suggestions and questions as individual teachers or in collaborative teams to support your work and conversations around implementing the FRAME model.

- Write your learning intention and success criteria for your upcoming lesson. How does your instruction or the way you teach change when you scaffold your lesson?

- The quality and clarity of the learning intention and success criteria are necessary for student success. Explain your process for ensuring both.

- Student-friendly language is critical when creating a learning intention and success criteria. How do you determine your language is student friendly?

- Think of a recent lesson you taught in which you gave students choices. How did students' choice impact the level of their engagement? What effect did choice have on their motivation?

CHAPTER 2

How to FRAME the First Ten Minutes of Class

How you use your time during the first several minutes of class, and before class even begins, can either inspire or tire. If you appear poorly prepared, without a process or a plan, your students might think your class is too easy or irrelevant, which could imply that the teacher's expectations are just too low. For example, in *The Opportunity Myth*, The New Teacher Project (2018) finds:

> . . . students reported that their school experiences were engaging just 55 percent of the time overall (among high schoolers, only 42 percent of the time). Underlying these weak experiences were low expectations: We found that while more than 80 percent of teachers supported standards for college readiness in theory, less than half had the expectation that their students could reach that bar.

This is alarming, to say the least. When teachers don't have a process or a plan, they are, in essence, telling their students that they really don't believe those students can reach a heightened level of success. This is extremely detrimental to students' learning. As The New Teacher Project (2018) further states, "Students spent more than 500 hours per school year on assignments that weren't appropriate for their grade and with instruction that didn't ask enough of them—the equivalent of six months of wasted class time in each core subject."

The report goes on to say that students who received work appropriate for their grade rose to the occasion more often than not, which infers that students fall behind when they don't have "access to four key resources: grade-appropriate assignments, strong instruction, deep engagement, and teachers who hold high expectations" (The New Teacher Project, 2018).

Providing a structured protocol for the first ten minutes of class aids students in knowing what to expect, thereby eliminating a key cause of students' anxiety. In providing these clear expectations, teachers establish an academic family built on supportive relationships. "When teachers identify and communicate clear learning objectives, they send the message that there is a focus for the learning activities to come. This reassures students that there is a reason for the learning" (Dean, Hubbell, Pitler, & Stone, 2012, p. 2).

At first glance, implementing FRAME in the first ten minutes of *every* class might seem daunting and challenging, especially if you teach within a thirty-five- to fifty-minute time frame. This is precisely why it's important to adapt FRAME to your unique teaching environment. Perhaps you need a couple of extra minutes beyond ten. Or, perhaps you don't need to implement every component of FRAME during every class. Perhaps you introduce each FRAME component at the beginning of a unit, but during every class period thereafter (for that unit), you forgo the ask component because the learning intention and success criteria haven't changed. Instead, you spend more time on the model component so students can see the various processes of the entire product.

Much as FRAME presents a structured protocol, what makes FRAME unique is the flexibility within that system to allow a teacher to design a class based on what his or her students need. So, as you implement FRAME, consider its purpose. Then, determine how you want to use it. As you introduce a new unit in your classroom, utilize all components of FRAME purposefully. But, as the work continues in class, determine the FRAME components that you and your students need most and focus on applying those. The implementation of FRAME will bring a structured sense of intentional calm to your classroom, but you are the expert on the environment and needs in your classroom, and you can and should adapt FRAME to fit that.

With this established, let's examine each of the FRAME components and how you can make the best use of them in the first ten minutes of your class. You'll then look at an example of FRAME at work in an exemplary classroom and review some do-now suggestions for your classroom or collaborative team.

Focus

As you learned in chapter 1 (page 13), producing a quality learning intention and success criteria require thoughtful planning. The learning intention focuses on the goal of the learning—the thing we want our students to know and be able to do. It helps students stay focused and involved, which helps to create a supportive classroom. According to Moss et al. (2011), "Students who don't know the intention of a lesson expend precious time and energy trying to figure out what their teachers expect them to learn. And many students, exhausted by the process, wonder why they should even care."

When students don't care about their learning, the classroom culture suffers. There is no sense of community; rather, students are apathetic about learning, and ultimately, according to Fisher and Frey (2018), "Without a clear learning destination in mind, lessons wander, and students become confused and frustrated" (p. 82).

As I wrote in chapter 1, teachers should devote time and significant thought to planning the learning intention and success criteria as they create and prepare for a lesson—before their students walk through the classroom door. Introducing the learning intention and success criteria in class also requires planning. Teachers must deliberately make decisions about where they will display the learning intention and success criteria (such as in a *welcome corner*) and how they will introduce them to focus students as class begins. The following sections will discuss how you can make these decisions.

Plan Ahead

Take the time to develop the learning intention and success criteria before students arrive; do not wait until the first several minutes of class to begin working on these foundational pieces. When teachers wait to do this, it looks to students as though the learning intention and success criteria are afterthoughts—as if the teacher just thought of them and had to hurriedly write them on the board. The day before you plan to deliver the lesson in question, consider spending time after the final bell crafting the next day's learning intention and success criteria with your content-area or grade-level colleagues. You can share ideas, propose suggestions, and offer critical analyses to create the best learning intention and success criteria for your students.

Prominently Display the Learning Intention and Success Criteria

Displaying the learning intention and success criteria in the same place every day helps your students know where to go to answer the first question they usually have when they come to class: "What are we doing today?" Beginning each day with a clear description of what they will be expected to know and do gets students poised and prepared for learning. According to *Classroom Instruction That Works*, "When teachers communicate objectives for student learning, students can see more easily the connections between what they are doing in class and what they are supposed to learn" (Dean, Hubbell, Pitler, & Stone, 2012, p. 3).

If you move the learning intention and success criteria to different areas of the room (displaying them sometimes in the front of the room, sometimes on a sidewall, and sometimes in the back corner), students might assume that the learning intention and success criteria aren't really that important. It gives students the impression that the learning intention and success criteria are just words that the teacher says at the start of class and aren't really relevant to *them*. Creating a specific location tells your students that the learning intention and success criteria are important to their learning and specifically designed for them. Creating a particular place of importance tells students you have put thought into their learning and you have expectations of success.

The front of the room is the best focal point for the learning intention and success criteria. Do not put the learning intention and the success criteria in the back of the classroom, where students can easily ignore them. Having the learning intention and success criteria in the front of the room ensures everyone can see and reference them throughout the lesson. If possible, the learning intention and success criteria should remain posted for the entire lesson so teachers and students can refer to them as often as necessary. Therefore, it's best to post them on a large sheet of paper, as opposed to on the chalkboard, where you might have to erase them, or on a digital display, which you might have to minimize.

Create a Welcome Corner

Consider creating a welcome corner and using this space in the classroom to display the day's learning intention and success criteria on butcher paper. Having a welcome corner helps students consistently locate the learning intention and success criteria. The space can also serve to reduce student anxiety by giving them a comfortable spot to relax. If you have room, add a beanbag chair and a cushion that can provide comfort and a quiet space.

The welcome corner is also a good place to display inspirational quotes that students find personally meaningful. Before the end of each day, ask for a student volunteer (do not assign this task) who wants to choose an inspirational message to hang in the welcome corner for the next day. Remember, this is meant to be a chance for students to share who they are with the class—their traditions, culture, or sense of humor. Encourage as many voices as possible to help create that classroom community. If you find that students aren't sure how to choose a quote, suggest they consider choosing a family adage that has been passed down from generation to generation, a message from someone the student admires, or an original proverb the student has created. Even a favorite song lyric, book passage, or movie quote is fertile ground for students' self-expression.

Imagine the pride the student will feel when he or she gets to read his or her posted inspirational message aloud at the beginning of the next class. The student can explain the significance of the message and share its background with his or her classmates. Having students share quotes that are meaningful to them helps encourage the supportive classroom culture of an academic family. In "Culture in the Classroom," Willis Hawley, Jacqueline Jordan Irvine, and Melissa Landa (n.d.) write, "To engage students effectively in the learning process, teachers must know their students and their academic abilities individually, rather than relying on racial or ethnic stereotypes or prior experience with other students of similar backgrounds." The welcome corner gives students the opportunity to share who they are, not who they are perceived to be.

Introduce the Learning Intention and Success Criteria

The bell has rung, and students are in their seats ready to begin the day's lesson. Although this process occurs during the ask component of the framework, it is essential to plan for it ahead of time, making it also a part of the focus component. At this point, there are several ways a teacher can plan to introduce the learning intention and success criteria to students.

- The teacher can read the learning intention and success criteria to the class where they are prominently displayed on large-print poster paper.

- The teacher can ask for a student volunteer to read the learning intention and success criteria displayed on a large piece of poster paper.

- If students sit in collaborative groups at tables or in pods, the teacher can give the learning intention and success criteria to each group on a piece of cardstock, and students can read them within their groups.

Especially in the early stages of using FRAME, I recommend that the teacher read the learning intention and success criteria to the class. According to Laura Varlas (2018), "Read alouds can draw students of any age into a community that is knowledgeable and curious about topics and texts, from novels to news reports." In her article, she further emphasizes that read alouds create class bonds and are ideal for previewing information. When the teacher reads the learning intention and success criteria, it helps model for students a common experience, a sense that this work is within their ability and all of them can do it. The reason for having the teacher conduct this process is that his or her use of tone, inflection, and emphasis can help create a fluent and clear understanding of what he or she expects of students. As students become increasingly familiar with a teacher's use of FRAME in the classroom, he or she can start opening up this introduction to cement further their engagement with it.

Reach

Teachers implement the reach component for two to three minutes as students are walking into the room, *prior* to the bell ringing to begin class. In many traditional classrooms, after the bell has rung, teachers commonly offer a whole-class "Good morning!" greeting. While courteous, that whole-class greeting can seem generic and seldom builds a community of learners, or more specifically, an academic family. Instead, give students individual time with you so they know you care about them as distinct members of your class. John Hattie (2012) reminds teachers, "A positive, caring, respectful climate in the classroom is a prior condition to learning" (p. 70). Therefore, to truly improve student learning, you must create relationships before your students walk into your classroom. These relationships form an academic family whose members come to rely on each other for care, compassion, and connection and rely on you for structure, advice, kindness, empathy, and when necessary, authority. So, don't wait until the bell has rung to create your family; begin building it before students even cross the threshold. This also gives you the space to focus on the *ask*, *model*, and *encourage* parts of the framework within the first official ten minutes of class.

Make it a point—a habit—to intentionally stand at the door prior to your students' entering the room. Greeting students before the bell has rung gives teachers a practical and reasonable way to create community. According to researchers Clayton R. Cook et al. (2018), greeting students at the door shows "significant improvements in academic engaged time and reductions in disruptive behavior" (p. 149). When students feel seen and welcomed in the classroom, they are more apt to put time and effort into their learning.

It is commonplace in classrooms for teachers to respond to misbehavior with corrective discipline, something that consumes both valuable time and energy (Terada, 2018). Greeting students at the door, however, can help curb that misbehavior. Cook (n.d.) goes on to say:

> Research and practical experience tells us that students are more engaged and better behaved in classrooms in which there is an upbeat climate and students feel that they have a positive relationship with their teacher. One easy and effective way to address this problem is to greet students at the door in a positive, intentional, and strategic way.

Students behave better when they walk into a classroom where they have received an individual greeting—a moment or two to have the teacher's attention all to themselves. According to Amelia Harper (2018), "The approach promotes a sense of belonging in the classroom, builds a sense of community, and reduces students' and teachers' stress levels as they begin the day."

As you stand outside your classroom door before the bell rings, have your attendance roster in hand, and check students off as they walk in, acknowledging every student's presence. For each student, offer the following.

- An engaging smile

- Individual eye contact

- The student's preferred name

- A simple "How are you today?"

- An individual handshake, pat on the back, or fist bump

Verbally letting your students know you care about them is essential; in addition, physically acknowledging their presence demonstrates you are happy to have them as important members of your classroom community. PBIS Rewards (n.d.) explains, "When you greet your students at the door, you are modeling the behaviors that you expect in the classroom. What's more, you're modeling adult behaviors expected in the larger community." As a result, standing at the door models for students a valuable social skill that is becoming increasingly important in our diverse society, where civil discourse—verbal or physical—can seem difficult to find (Wan, 2018; Zeman, 2015).

When you greet your students at the door, that simple "Hello" with a follow-up question, or the compliment about the student's new hat, or praise for the student who came to school on time or showed outstanding work ethic the previous day—all of those little instances that we often perceive as minor—you are, in fact, embracing major opportunities to reach out and model kindness and compassion to your students.

Ask

The ask component marks the start of in-class time. During the ask component, the teacher takes four to five minutes to familiarize students with the learning intention and success criteria that he or she posted before class began. In the Focus section (page 37), I wrote about how you must decide ahead of time how you are going to read (or have read) the learning intention and success criteria, but in practice, it's important to do more than just read them. This is when you give students the opportunity to dig deeper into the expectations. The ask component of the FRAME model builds in time for students to truly examine the learning intention and success criteria. They can ask questions, paraphrase the learning intention and success criteria, analyze the expectations of the task, discuss their ideas with their peers, and share feedback. This is the students' opportunity to get crystal clarity on what is being asked of them. Moss et al. (2011) explain the importance of this clarity when they write, "Regardless of how important the content, how engaging the activity, how formative the assessment, or how differentiated the instruction, unless *all students* see, recognize, and understand the learning target from the very beginning of the lesson, one factor will remain constant: The teacher will always be the only one providing the direction . . ."

Encouraging students to ask questions about the learning intention and success criteria and paraphrase the learning intention and success criteria in pairs or small groups will also motivate them because it will help them understand what you are asking them to do. WestEd (n.d.) explains, "Students learn better when they know what is expected of them. They are more motivated to learn when they know where they are going" (p. 5). The learning intention and success criteria are meant to guide the purpose of the lesson.

Every teacher knows that a common roadblock to classroom engagement is students disrupting learning for other students. Rachel Ehmke (n.d.), the managing editor at the Child Mind Institute, writes, "When kids start noticing that something is harder for them than the other kids, and that they are falling behind, they can understandably get anxious." This anxiety can lead to negative behavior. As Ehmke (n.d.) further states, "Acting out is another thing we might not associate with anxiety. . . . Anxiety can also make kids aggressive. When children are feeling upset or threatened and don't know how to handle their feelings, their fight or flight response to protect themselves can kick in—and some kids are more likely to fight." So it follows that reducing anxiety about learning in students can help inhibit disruptive behavior before it starts.

By asking questions and paraphrasing the learning intention and success criteria in pairs or small groups, students can work together to determine what makes sense and what doesn't. This preparation helps to prevent the anxiety that could otherwise occur during the lesson. Researcher Sharon B. Kletzien (2009) reminds teachers that paraphrasing helps students "make connections with prior knowledge" (p. 73) and "translate the material to their own way of saying it" (p. 73). If students can paraphrase the learning intention in their own words—words they understand—they will have a greater chance of understanding and succeeding in the work.

Additionally, when students paraphrase the learning intention and success criteria, it gives teachers the chance to discover what their students know or understand about the learning intention. Scholastic Teachers blogger Meghan Everette (2017) recommends teachers "ask students to discuss the objective when [teachers] start the lesson, telling what they already know and what they are confused about." If students find paraphrasing the learning intention a challenge, this could indicate a gap in the students' learning. Based on student responses, the teacher will be able to scaffold the lesson for students who seem unsure. For example, as students prepare to read *Macbeth* (Shakespeare, 1993) for sophomore English, the learning intention might be, *I can analyze how characters interact with each other and show how those interactions advance Macbeth's motives.*

After the teacher has read the learning intention to the students, she asks students to take out a piece of paper and pick out three or four words from the learning intention that they think are important. She gives the students thirty seconds to write down their list. Most students jot down the words *analyze, interact, advance,* and *motives.* Then, she asks students to write down a synonym or two-word phrase next to the list of important words and gives students another thirty seconds. Students write down synonyms, such as the following.

- **Analyze:** Break apart, tear down
- **Interact:** Discuss, connect
- **Advance:** Move forward, keep going
- **Motives:** Impulse, the cause

Finally, she gives students roughly sixty to ninety seconds to work in groups of three or four and use their synonyms to construct a paraphrased learning intention. Some of their examples include: *I can take apart how characters connect with each other and how those connections move Macbeth's reasons forward,* and *I can break apart the characters' personalities and show how their discussions with Macbeth show his impulsive nature.*

After students have created a paraphrased learning intention, they can share it with the class verbally, or they can attach their paraphrased learning intention to the one the teacher wrote. It can be especially powerful to show the different paraphrased learning intentions surrounding the teacher's learning intention because it signifies to students that while the language may change, the overall goal of what their teacher wants them to know and be able to do is the same.

If you're concerned about how you might help students who are struggling to paraphrase prompts, consider the following example learning intentions from chapter 1 (pages 18–20), and how you might encourage students to paraphrase them.

- **Second-grade mathematics:**
  - *Learning intention*—I can understand the place value of numbers up to 1,000.
  - *Paraphrasing suggestions*—
    - I can learn where to put the numbers in the right order.
    - I can figure out how to write numbers in the right order.

- **Third-grade reading:**
  - *Learning intention*—I can find and tell the main idea of the texts read in class and share examples with my peers.
  - *Paraphrasing suggestions*—
    - I can figure out the main idea of what we're reading and show my friends the main idea.
    - I can find the main idea in the books I'm reading and show my group.

- **Sixth- to eighth-grade science and technical subjects:**
  - *Learning intention*—I can learn the differences among superstition, pseudoscience, and science.
  - *Paraphrasing suggestions*—
    - I can look up, learn about, and explain the differences among the terms superstition, pseudoscience, and science.
    - I know the differences among superstition, pseudoscience, and science, and I can explain them.

- **Eighth-grade U.S. history:**
  - *Learning intention*—I can discuss, explain, and research the events leading to the American Revolution and their influence on the formation of the Constitution.

- *Paraphrasing suggestions*—
  - I can talk about, describe, and look up the events leading to the American Revolution and their effect on the creation of the Constitution.
  - I can communicate, describe, and investigate the events leading to the American Revolution and their impact on the development of the Constitution.

- **Ninth- and tenth-grade English language arts:**
  - *Learning intention*—I can understand the role and proper use of figurative language in a narrative.
  - *Paraphrasing suggestions*—
    - I can define figurative language and understand why it's important.
    - I can explain figurative language and how it's used in the books I'll read.

- **Eleventh- and twelfth-grade writing:**
  - *Learning intention*—I can write an argument to support a claim using valid reasoning and relevant and sufficient evidence.
  - *Paraphrasing suggestions*—
    - I can write an argument to support something I believe in and use logical reasoning with adequate evidence to back up what I want to prove.
    - I can write an argument to support my point using practical reasoning and satisfactory evidence.

Students can paraphrase the learning intention individually or in pairs or small groups. Pairs and groups lend themselves to deeper conversations about the language and its meaning. In addition, it might support your students to have them use a thesaurus as they are looking up the important words in the learning intention. Not only will they be paraphrasing the learning intention to assure understanding, but they might also increase their vocabulary in the process! After pairs or small groups have paraphrased the learning intention, give students a chance to talk with their peers about how they will tackle each step of the success criteria. Consider these same steps when asking students to paraphrase the success criteria. You may find that students don't necessarily need to break down the success criteria since it has been scaffolded for them; however, it is always important to ensure that your students understand the directive language and that they can act upon that language. Encourage students to share their ideas about what they will need to do to successfully meet both the learning intention and success criteria so their peers can consider, use, or adapt their suggestions.

According to Everette (2017), "Having students take ownership of their own learning happens when they can talk about what they are learning, why they are learning it, and how they will know when they are successful." In other words, don't merely ask students if they "get it" or ask them for a proverbial thumbs-up, thumbs-down, or thumbs-sideways. Sometimes, students might say they get it just so the teacher stops talking, or they may just go with the majority of their peers. Instead, the ask component of the FRAME model urges you and your students to slow down and not leap into the content quite yet. It gives you an opportunity to check for understanding. It gives students a chance to familiarize themselves with the content and understand the expectations for their learning. Most important, it gives students a chance to breathe and realize that the learning intention and success criteria are meant to hone their skills as learners.

Model

During the model component, the teacher takes four to five minutes to share the process for meeting each of the success criteria, actively *showing* students the learning progressions necessary to be successful. (Refer to Using Learning Progressions, page 21, if you need a refresher on these.) If you only *tell* students how to approach the work, very few of them will understand. Telling isn't modeling. Telling isn't instruction. You must demonstrate the pieces of the process for ultimate understanding and follow up with explicit instruction for student success.

It may seem hard to imagine covering this process in just a few minutes, so let's look at an example. During this initial model step, the teacher can show students an example of each scaffolded success criteria. For example, we can use the *Macbeth* (Shakespeare, 1993) example from the Ask section (page 42): *I can analyze how characters interact with each other and show how those interactions advance Macbeth's motives.* The teacher can show students a handout with two characters, Macbeth and Lady Macbeth. Then, the teacher can show two or three examples of evidence from the play where the characters are talking to each other and reacting to something the other has said. The final example the teacher shows illustrates evidence aligned to Macbeth's desire for advancement. For these first ten minutes of class, the modeling stage is not about giving students the entire meal (which will come during the full-class instruction), but rather an appetizer to give them a taste of what they will be doing.

However brief this step, don't give in to the temptation to merely show the finished product. It's important to show multiple examples that highlight the milestones along the learning journey. Students must know they can successfully achieve the learning intention and understand the learning progressions that lead to meeting each of the success criteria. Teacher modeling of the full process toward creating the product will support their achievement. The key is to model in such a way that causes students to "picture themselves following the precise path you create for them" (Linsin, 2015). They must be able to visualize completing each specific step before it becomes a reality.

Equally important is to be unambiguous in your instruction. Students will become frustrated if they do not understand how they can eventually reach the conclusion of a process. Show students the work they will have to produce to create a final product or some other assignment. Also consider using the "Bloom's Taxonomy Verb Chart" (Shabatu, 2018) to ensure you use with them the kinds of robust verbs, precise language, and specificity that should highlight their own work. If your language is unclear, imprecise, or ambiguous, your students will not know what they need to know and be able to do. You must become purposeful in your modeling and definitive in your instruction so your students learn.

As part of this step, remind students that learning is a process and part of that process is seeing examples of the work they will do. WestEd (n.d.) explains, "Often it is useful to show examples of students' work (not from the same class) as a means to make the criteria clear" (p. 5). Students must be able to recognize that they can successfully complete the learning intention. Illustrate the process by showing students an example of each step of the success criteria, and name each learning progression for accuracy and understanding. Then, show them the completed task. When students see this, they will realize that they, too, can be successful.

According to Landmark Outreach Staff (2017):

> Creating and improvising opportunities to involve students in the learning process allows students to become aware of *how* they learn and *why* certain skills benefit them. As a result, students are motivated and more likely to apply those skills when working independently. In short, an included student becomes an invested student who is eager to learn.

When you exhibit various phases of student work, students see the progression of skills and realize that they, too, can move from one skill to another. For example, when highlighting modeling and instruction in mathematics, show the process of how to solve a problem, and utilize rich, precise mathematics vocabulary to help students see and hear the process. In this case, briefly show students the process of first underlining and defining a main word; then, using the vocabulary, rephrase what the problem is asking the student to do; and finally solve the problem utilizing what the student has already done. Once students see the scope of the process they are to undertake—identifying the main idea, paraphrasing the directions, and solving the problem—they will understand how they can apply this strategy not only to mathematics but to other subjects as well.

This transfer of learning to other academic disciplines doesn't happen automatically, however. Unfortunately, students don't necessarily transfer what they learned in one context to new contexts (Darling-Hammond & Austin, n.d.), and as a result, students have a habit of compartmentalizing their learning. According to the Eberly Center (n.d.), from Carnegie Mellon University, "Students often don't see the relevance of prior material because they compartmentalize knowledge by course, semester, professor, or discipline and so they don't even think to bring that knowledge to bear." For example, students may naturally write in a more sophisticated way in English class than in an art class. Students perceive that the English teacher will be strict regarding the nuances of English, whereas the art teacher won't necessarily check grammar, mechanics, or syntax.

To counteract this effect and push students to think broader about their learning, teachers should use the model component to highlight similarities in skills among classes. For example, a teacher might demonstrate that creating a claim in English is similar to forming a hypothesis in science, or highlight that in-text citations are necessary when proving one's point in all well-written papers, regardless of the subject.

Using the analytical essay as an example, the teacher can use a SMART Board to show the various pieces that go into the final product: the brainstorming worksheet; rough draft; thesis paragraph; first, second, and third body paragraphs; and conclusion. The final step is to show a completed essay. By viewing these pieces, the students can see that the various components form a completed paper. According to researchers Kristin E. Harbour, Lauren L. Evanovich, Chris A. Sweigart, and Lindsay E. Hughes (2015), "Modeling decreases student error, positively affects the perceived importance of a task and increases self-regulated learning" (as cited in Educational Research Newsletter & Webinars, 2015). During this procedure, students can determine their level of comfort or trepidation with the steps of the process. Some students might feel energized by this task and look forward to the challenge that it entails. However, other students may feel nervous about the writing task and realize they may need more support in the process. They can share their concern with the teacher, giving the teacher the chance to support the student with extra practice or peer assistance.

Encourage

During the encourage component, the teacher takes one to two minutes to encourage a growth mindset prior to the lesson he or she is teaching. According to researcher Carol Dweck (n.d.), when people have a growth mindset, they believe that "their most basic abilities can be developed through dedication and hard work—brains and talent are just the starting point. This view creates a love of learning and a resilience that is essential for great accomplishment."

After completing the modeling component, but prior to beginning the lesson, let students know you trust their ability to learn the material you just outlined for them. Don't praise how smart they are; instead, emphasize the *worthwhile effort* they will be putting forward to achieve the learning intention, and assure them that this effort may come with challenges or even setbacks but will ultimately translate into real growth. Dweck advises, "Praise the effort that led to the outcome or learning progress; tie the praise to it. It's not just effort, but strategy . . . so support the student in finding another strategy" (as quoted in Gross-Loh, 2016).

In addition, the encouragement you provide must be specific and connected to the modeling work you just completed. According to Emily Richards (n.d.):

> If one of the primary goals of praise is to encourage good work, then praise should include information about what exactly good work is. Only when they know what they did well can students make sure to repeat their success.

To further ensure clarity on what constitutes good work, you may choose to employ an instrument of growth such as a rubric. Whatever method you decide on, be clear with students about their level of achievement. Richards (n.d.) explains, "When teachers talk up students' achievements but become silent in the face of failure, the message is: Failure is too shameful to talk about." Let your students know this work will be hard and they might need to make revisions or perhaps even do it over again. Also, take the opportunity to let students know you will conduct discussions centered on their learning and that you will always encourage them to go back and try again. However, when discussing students' strengths and challenges, make sure you use language that focuses on the process rather than the person. Positive psychology specialist Kathryn Britton (2007) recommends using *process praise*, which focuses on the effort or strategy behind a specific behavior. Process praise targets students' determination, the strategies they used, or their collaboration with their peers. According to Britton (2007), "Process praise tends to be motivating, to increase self-confidence, and to lead to mastery behavior, while person praise promotes avoidance of challenges and greater fear of failure." Having those individual conversations with students about their achievement level and process shows that you care about the students and how they can move forward in the face of adversity. Developmental psychologist Allison Master (2015) explains:

> Process praise that emphasizes students' effort or strategy is more likely to lead to resilient responses after negative feedback or failure. Children can still feel positive emotions even after mistakes, because their value as a person hasn't been called into question. (p. 2)

With process praise, mistakes become opportunities to learn and try again, instead of devastating setbacks where the student feels defeated and demoralized.

In addition, let students know that you have chosen work that you specifically designed for them, not work that might be considered irrelevant or inconsequential busywork. You have designed a lesson that will support their curiosity to become global learners. So tell students that they may find the work difficult and struggle to understand it, but as members of an academic family, they will have support within the classroom community to understand the learning intention and apply it. As a result, no learner will be left behind, and all students will move forward.

Also, stay away from empty language that doesn't support students and the work they are doing. As an example, psychology expert Jim Taylor (2009) contends that the phrase *good job* is "lazy praise, it's worthless praise, it's harmful praise. It has no value to children, yet parents have been brainwashed into thinking that it will build their children's self-esteem. Plus, it's the expedient thing to say." Instead of generically saying, "Good job," consider using thoughtful praise that benefits the process and helps build learning confidence, such as the following examples.

- "I know that took a lot of time and work, but you stuck to it and accomplished the goals for this lesson."

- "What strategy have you already used? How did it help you? Which one should we try now?"

- "I noticed the results improved from your last test. What did you do differently this time?"

- "I noticed you stayed at your desk and kept working on this problem even though it was challenging. I appreciate your sticking with it."

In helping students develop a growth mindset, praise should be all about the learning, not about the learner. Take the opportunity to praise the work students are doing, but be careful of praising the individual.

The Exemplary Classroom

On the first day of the new school year, I introduced FRAME in my own classroom to my middle school students. This first day was a shortened period due to other scheduled programs. I (literally!) framed the FRAME acronym in my classroom's welcome corner, located in the front corner of my room. There, I also placed beanbag chairs and cushions to provide a comfortable spot where students could read and relax. I established my routine of reaching out to each student by standing at my door with my attendance roster. As students walked in, I asked them to pronounce their name for me. I shook each student's hand and, pronouncing students' names as they had, made sure to greet students individually, saying, "Good morning," and thanking each of them for coming.

When students entered the classroom for the first time, I let them sit wherever they wanted. Then, I explained the purpose of FRAME's focus component and why it is important. I walked over to the big piece of poster paper hanging on the side wall of my classroom and explained this is where they would always find the learning intention and the success criteria. I explained I would always write the learning intention and success criteria the day before and hang it up in the welcome corner for them to read after they walked in from their greeting with me. I also explained that I would always read it to them. Finally, I explained that the learning intention and success criteria would tell them what the lesson would be for that particular day; it would tell them the concepts and skills they would need to know and eventually be able to do. I read the following learning intention and success criteria for that day.

- **Learning intention:** I can explain the purpose of the focus component and be an active listener as I learn about my classroom community.

- **Success criteria:** I know I am successful because—
    1. I can explain the purpose of the focus component
    2. I can list three things I learned about my classroom community

You will note that this day's lesson was not academic, but rather an opportunity to begin to build a classroom community. For the first day of class, I recommend you begin with a structure that will ultimately help students be successful. FRAME is that structured approach.

Next, I implemented the ask component of FRAME. I explained that we would be starting every class with FRAME and I wanted to introduce what the first ten minutes of our class would always look like. I distributed a piece of paper to each student. I explained we were going to paraphrase the learning intention first so all students would understand what they were to know and be able to do. I asked students to write down what they perceived to be the important words of the learning intention. Then, I asked them to jot down a synonym next to those important words. Next, I asked students to paraphrase the learning intention. I gave them ninety seconds to do this work. I did not ask students to work in pairs or in small groups since this was our first day of class. Next, I asked for volunteers to share their examples. One student read her learning intention, which was, "I can explain why the learning intention and success criteria are important and meet other people." Another student said, "I can explain the focus and get to know my classmates."

Giving students another ninety seconds, we replicated the process for the success criteria. I asked for a volunteer to share his or her success criteria, and a student replied, "I know I am successful because I can explain the reason for focus and I can learn about my classroom community." Another student asked why he should paraphrase if he understood the success criteria. I explained there would be no reason to. But while others were practicing their paraphrasing, could he jot down examples of what he was going to do to meet the success criteria? We spent four minutes on the ask portion of FRAME, including student responses.

Then, I explained we would move on to the modeling component of FRAME. This is where I would demonstrate an example of the process of how we might learn our success criteria. I showed students a brief, three-sentence paragraph about the importance of knowing what we were going to study; then, I modeled the introductions by walking around the classroom and talking to two students and asking a question to get to know them. The model component of FRAME took about four minutes. Finally, I explained the last part of FRAME—encouragement. For two minutes, I briefly shared what a growth mindset is and why it is important and how I believe in the capacity of every student in the room to learn and thrive. I also explained that we would be talking a lot about process and why it is important.

As you can see, in this scenario, I successfully applied the FRAME components during the first ten minutes of class. To carry out FRAME during the rest of our abbreviated class, I had students fulfill the modeling portion by writing a brief three-sentence paragraph on what they thought the purpose of FRAME would be for our class. Then, I asked students to get up and introduce themselves to three classmates and ask one question. When they were finished meeting their peers, I asked them to take their seats and write down three things they learned about their classroom community. I asked students to turn in their papers to me when the bell rang. Later that day, as I wrote my learning intention and success criteria on poster paper for the next day, I taped their responses to the paper. I wanted them to see the various responses they had created and made their responses a key focus of the next day's plan.

Conclusion

FRAME is all about establishing routine and structure before students enter the room and in those critical first few minutes as class begins. It's about building community in an authentic and relevant way, showing students how to ask questions and analyze the learning they will be doing, modeling the process and the product, supporting students in using strategies, and encouraging productive struggle so students learn and grow. In this way, FRAME supports all learners of all grade levels and all abilities in respectful and honorable ways.

Do-Now Suggestions for Your Classroom or Collaborative Team

Reflect on the following suggestions and questions as individual teachers or in collaborative teams to support your work and conversations around implementing the FRAME model.

- As you consider implementing FRAME for the first ten minutes of your class, what do you think might be your biggest challenge?

- The learning intention and success criteria are a vital component of the FRAME model. How will you assure that the learning intention and success criteria will be ready? Will you write it the night before class? In the morning before class?

- Why do you think paraphrasing is so vital to the FRAME component?

- How does modeling help to alleviate student anxiety?

- Jot down a few examples of how you could implement process praise to your students during the lesson. How could you incorporate language that supports a growth mindset when you encourage student progress?

CHAPTER 3

How to Embed FRAME Within a Lesson

After teachers have implemented FRAME during the first ten minutes of class, they should continue utilizing this model throughout the lesson. Students want the same kind of structure for the remainder of the class, giving them opportunities to relate and reflect on the learning with their teacher, their peers, and themselves. As author and educator Melissa Kelly (2019) reminds teachers, "Every teacher must develop classroom procedures in order to . . . create a more effective learning environment for students." When teachers implement FRAME, they implement procedures consistently; ensuring students become comfortable with the structure. In *Creating Classroom Routines and Procedures*, Scholastic (n.d.) states:

> When routines and procedures are carefully taught, modeled, and established in the classroom, children know what's expected of them and how to do certain things on their own. Having these predictable patterns in place allows teachers to spend more time in meaningful instruction.

FRAME promotes meaningful instruction by establishing such routines and procedures. Saga Briggs (2014), the managing editor of InformED, explains, "Simply put, when a teacher provides relevance for a student, the teacher conveys his or her intentions to the student by tapping into that student's cognitive need to make sense of the world." Further, the Department of Education and Training (2017) reports, "Effective teachers plan and deliver structured lessons which incorporate a series of clear steps and transitions between them, and scaffold learning to build students' knowledge and skills" (p. 13). These *clear steps* are the learning intention and success criteria that explain to students what they are supposed to know and be able to do.

However, while the structure is indeed important for optimal learning, especially during the first ten minutes of class, teachers don't need to embed the FRAME model as explicitly throughout the class as during those first ten minutes. Teachers can apply all or some of the FRAME components during the lesson; this gives them the flexibility to spend more time or less time on a single component, depending on what students need. This chapter focuses on how teachers can most effectively use each FRAME component to conduct an entire lesson over the course of a class. It concludes with an example from an exemplary classroom and a series of do-now suggestions for teachers or collaborative teams.

Focus

In the FRAME model, focusing students on the learning intention and success criteria continues throughout the lesson. During the lesson, it's important that the teacher review the learning intention and the learning progressions within the success criteria on an as-needed basis, throughout the lesson, to ensure students confidently work toward these criteria.

In this regard, teachers must use their judgment on when to direct students back to the learning intention and success criteria throughout a lesson. For example, if the teacher observes off-task student behaviors, then it is time to bring student attention to the learning intention and success criteria. As the teacher listens to small group conversations, give students the opportunity to offer success criteria exemplars as a means to gauge if students are showing comprehension of the learning intention and success criteria. This is an ongoing process, and teachers will grow more comfortable knowing when to re-engage students' focus as they get to know their students. In many cases, a review of the learning intention and success criteria could be as simple as rereading them to the class or asking two or three students to read the paraphrased learning intention and success criteria they wrote during the ask component in the first ten minutes of class.

Throughout the following pages, you will see more ways teachers can focus the student back to the learning intention and success criteria. Examples include reaching out to each student, asking students to clarify their understanding and analyze their comprehension, and modeling the pieces of the success criteria. Teachers and students shouldn't only focus on the learning intention and success criteria during the first ten minutes of class; rather, teachers should make this focus an ongoing topic of conversation so students always know whether they are on the right track toward their individual success.

Reach

In the context of a full class, reaching out to each student encompasses a variety of possibilities. The length of the teacher's contact time with each student is not important; what is vital is that each student experiences a meaningful connection with the teacher. Education journalist Holly Korbey (2017) suggests that "welcome rituals and routines, more engaging or interactive teaching methods, and end-of-class reflections" help teachers get to know their students and thereby create those personal opportunities for connection.

Although the possibilities for this are limitless, some common examples of engaging or interactive teaching methods include: Socratic seminars, stations, flipped classroom instruction, inquiry-based discussion, cooperative groups, and student movement. Todd Finley (2015) recommends some closure activities, such as snowstorm, sequence it, beat the clock, students I learned from the most, and out-the-door activity. Each of these activities, which you can learn more about with a quick internet search, creates opportunities for teachers to reach out quickly, briefly, and explicitly to make connections with students. In addition to these strategies, the following sections cover some of the methods I use every day when interacting with students—making eye contact, using students' names, and having conversations with students.

Eye Contact

A teacher implementing FRAME makes deliberate eye contact with students during the first ten minutes of class. However, once class begins, he or she may easily get caught up in the everyday housekeeping of directing a classroom and forget about intentionally engaging in this simple, obvious behavior. It's important that you continue making eye contact with students because it demonstrates your willingness to support them and your desire for high expectations. Linguistics expert Leila Barati (2015) explains that "longer eye contact is associated with trust, good feelings, and rapport [sic] all of which are important" (p. 224). Malik Amer Atta and Muhammad Ayaz (2014) further write:

> Eye contact convey our inner most warm thoughts and desires, it can let the students we are speaking with know our emotional connection and interest in what we are conversing about. The ability to smile with your eyes can often deliver a fine message of interest. (p. 92)

This "emotional connection" with students illustrates the high expectations all teachers have for their students. We want our students to do well, and eye contact delivers warmth and comfort to students who are often eager and sometimes desperate to have an adult figure in their lives who believes in them. This type of classroom culture creates a student-focused, academic family, which is the very foundation of FRAME. You want your class to be a place where students feel they can succeed; eye contact helps create and maintain those good feelings.

Student Names

Reaching out to a student during class by using the student's name may also seem obvious, but it is vital in building classroom relationships. According to researchers Katelyn M. Cooper, Brian Haney, Anna Krieg, and Sara E. Brownell (2017), "Learning student names has been promoted as an inclusive classroom practice." They go on to explain that "learning student names is frequently recommended as a simple instructional practice to build immediacy with students" and "students feel valued" when instructors know their names (Cooper et al., 2017). To learn names quickly, create a seating chart with students' pictures next to their names; then, you can visually connect the name with the student. Also, consider rehearsing student names.

As you commit your students' names to memory, you can begin to focus on the many ways you can incorporate them throughout a lesson in a natural way. As an example, most common is during questioning—when you ask a question, call on the student using his or her name. When returning papers, use student names and offer a positive comment, something that emphasizes that student's growth mindset as I detailed in chapter 2 (page 49). Another way to incorporate reach during your lesson is to always use student names when sharing good news or congratulations—birthdays, quinceañeras, athletic or academic news, fine arts concerts or shows—anything that will personalize the experience or situation for the student.

If you are having trouble pronouncing a student's name, respectfully ask the student to help you pronounce it correctly. Name mispronunciation is a *microaggression* (Furr,

2016), something researchers at Columbia University's Teachers College define as "brief and commonplace daily verbal, behavioral, or environmental indignities, whether intentional or unintentional, that communicate hostile, derogatory, or negative racial slights and insults toward people of color" (Sue et al., 2007, p. 271). Amy Furr (2016) also reports on University of California, Riverside research that clarifies that any form of mispronouncing, disregard to, or changes to a student's name shows a direct disregard for his or her family and culture.

Education writer Jennifer Gonzalez (2014) goes on to say:

> In other words, mutilating someone's name is a tiny act of bigotry. Whether you intend to or not, what you're communicating is this: Your name is different. Foreign. Weird. It's not worth my time to get it right. Although most of your students may not know the word *microaggression*, they're probably familiar with that vague feeling of marginalization, the message that everyone else is "normal," and they are not.

Therefore, when you are willing to practice saying a student's name so that you pronounce it accurately, it shows that you respect and revere that student and his or her culture. This seemingly small gesture lets the student know you are connecting directly with him or her, and you care about his or her culture, ethnicity, and familial background. Remember, your willingness to connect with (to *reach* out to) your students positively affects their learning. Students will appreciate your desire to want to get to know their name because getting to know their name is getting to know them.

Conversation

During the lesson, spend individualized time with each student based on his or her specific need to be successful. In the revised edition of *Poor Students, Rich Teaching*, education and poverty expert Eric Jensen (2019) demonstrates that, while all students have a need to connect, the degree to which any specific student may have that need met outside the classroom is highly variable. Often, the students who seem the most difficult to reach are those most desperate for a connection. Look for these students, and go out of your way to build even the most basic of connections with them. Although such conversations could focus on the important work the student is doing, do not ignore the opportunity to ask a safe personal question—questions that are not controversial or do not distract from the learning. While teachers want to get to know our students personally, it is important to respect personal boundaries. Asking safe personal questions helps to get to know students without overstepping the student-teacher relationship. As you become increasingly familiar with a student, you will mutually come to understand where the boundaries are.

Educator Michael Schultz (2015) recommends you "talk to [students] about their learning, but not just about their learning. Talk to them about what interests them outside of the world of academics." When teachers make the effort to learn more about their students and their students' hobbies and interests, they make and nurture personal connections. Schultz (2015) goes on to say that, when asked, most "students thought it was important to be able to talk to their teachers about their hobbies and their friends and what sorts of music they liked so that they could get to know them as people." This type of relationship is vital to building and maintaining an academic family. Once you have learned about students' activities and interests, consider bringing your family to attend a school football game, forensics meet, or musical to further build this academic family. These are sincere, personal ways to show your respect for the gifts and talents students have cultivated and admiration for the various social and emotional opportunities the school community offers to each student.

Harry K. Wong and Rosemary T. Wong (2018) remind teachers that when you "touch the life of a student . . . [that student] will also turn cartwheels to please and impress you with [his or her] success" (p. 18). The American Psychological Association also echoes the importance of relationships, saying, "Those students who have close, positive and supportive relationships with their teachers will attain higher levels of achievement than those students with more conflict in their relationships" (Rimm-Kaufman & Sandilos, n.d.).

With this in mind, it remains important to understand that there is a fine line between *teacher* and *buddy* as teachers make these gestures and hold conversations with students. Be careful not to become your students' best friend. Your role is one of teacher, mentor, and leader, and that is enough. Often, teachers—especially novice teachers—leave their expectations or rules a bit slack because they want their students to like them. While these teachers understand the value and importance of building relationships, finding and adhering to building those relationships can be difficult for a novice teacher. Teachers need to remember that they must implement structure before they can create a classroom community. As an example, brainstorm with your elementary and middle school students the classroom expectations that will create a community. For high school students, have your syllabus ready on that first day, but give them the opportunity to share with you and their peers how to make the classroom a positive place. Reaching out demonstrates your commitment to your students and their social-emotional learning. Always remember, you are not your students' friend; you are their teacher. Reach out and be the teacher and mentor they need and deserve.

Ask

During the first ten minutes of class, students had the opportunity to paraphrase the learning intention and success criteria and spend time talking about them, ensuring they understand what you expect them to do and learn. During the remaining class time, it is imperative that you continually pause to ask questions and analyze responses for clarity so you ensure that students understand the task in front of them. This often entails returning to the focus component of FRAME (page 56), but here we outline some other specific strategies to accomplish this: using clarifying and probing questions, one-to-one miniconferences, engagement forms, and self-assessment. Through these strategies, you engage students in forming and asking the kinds of questions necessary for them to accomplish their learning intention and all the success criteria associated with it.

Clarifying and Probing Questions

It's important to give your students the opportunity to practice asking questions, a skill that is vital for understanding and synthesizing information (Neal, 2011). This is essentially a form of *inquiry-based learning*, in which teachers induce students to be active participants in their own learning through the posing of questions, problems, and scenarios (as opposed to passively listening to a teacher stand and deliver learning content). About inquiry-based learning, Edutopia blogger Heather Wolpert-Gawron (2016) writes:

> When you ask a student something like, "What do you want to know about _____?" you're often met with a shrug or "Dunno." Inquiry-based learning, if front-loaded well, generates such excitement in students that neurons begin to fire, curiosity is triggered, and they can't wait to become experts in answering their own questions.

During the lesson, continue to ask questions and encourage conversation that inspires higher-order thinking. Critical-thinking questions give students a chance to highlight the process of the work and reflect on it. For example, ask students to explain the evidence of the work they're doing, analyze the patterns they notice within the work, or create other methods to do the work. These conversations are essential in creating a classroom of high expectations.

As an example, let's apply this specific strategy to a middle school mathematics class studying percentages in small groups. As the teacher moves throughout the room, reaching out to students, she asks them to connect with their peers. She chooses three students to mingle among the various other small groups in the classroom asking questions and gives them clarifying and probing question stems to facilitate their conversations with the various groups. As the students gather information, they share that information with other groups and eventually return to their own group. The teacher then designates three more students to do the same. These students become the facilitators and share what they are hearing and seeing with the other groups in class. Through this simple exercise, all students have an opportunity to practice reaching out in an engaging and motivating way.

The key to this process is the nature of the questions students are asking. In this section, we focus specifically on clarifying and probing questions as the best way to keep students engaged. *Clarifying questions* give students the chance to own their learning by helping them dig deeper into topics and concepts that interest them. They are "simple questions of fact. They clarify the dilemma and provide the nuts and bolts so that the participants can ask good probing questions and provide useful feedback" (Indiana University, 2013, p. 1). Examples of clarifying questions include:

- "Is this what you said . . . ?"
- "Did I understand you when you said . . . ?"
- "What's another way you might . . . ?"
- "Did I hear you correctly when you said . . . ?"
- "Did I paraphrase what you said correctly?" (Indiana University, 2013)

Probing questions are intended to help the student think more deeply. Examples of probing questions include the following (Indiana University, 2013).

- "Why do you think this is the case?"
- "What do you think would happen if . . . ?"
- "What sort of impact do you think _____ would have?"
- "How did you decide to . . . ?"
- "How did you accomplish . . . ?"
- "What is the connection between _____ and _____?"
- "What if the opposite were true?"
- "Imagine what would happen if . . . ?"

- "Do you agree with this statement, concept, or argument?
  Why or why not?"

Initially, these questions might seem a bit stiff. But students can practice them and substitute more personal language to make them their own. In addition, they certainly don't have to use all the clarifying or probing questions in their small groups; rather, encourage students to use the ones they feel comfortable with, thereby making the conversation more authentic and reflective.

In addition, students might need a little extra support in expressing comments that help deepen the work they are doing. The following comments help students unpack the layers of the work while collaborating with their peers in thoughtful and respectful ways. These stems give students more precise language in which to ask and analyze throughout the lesson.

- "I noticed . . ."
- "I predict . . ."
- "This reminds me of . . ."
- "I think . . ."
- "I'm surprised that . . ."
- "I'd like to know . . ."
- "I realized . . ."
- "If I were . . ."
- "I didn't know that . . ."

Clarifying and probing questions and insightful comments show students how to cooperate with each other, so they create a classroom community that focuses on collective success. As a means to give your students opportunities to reach out to you and each other, as you circulate throughout the classroom during the lesson, make sure your students are working toward their respective goals; you can do this by asking your own questions to check for student understanding and analyzing student work to determine comprehension. In addition, when preparing a lesson, try to build in time for students to ask questions of you and each other. Make questioning a priority in your classroom as you build a community of curiosity.

One-to-One Miniconferences

As students are working individually on a task, circulate throughout the classroom and hold short one-to-one miniconferences (no more than two to four minutes long), during which you ask questions to determine the student's progress on the success criteria. During the miniconference, ask the student to demonstrate or explain for you how he or she has met one component of the success criteria; use robust questions that help you determine if the student has met one or all of the components of the success criteria. According to Fisher and Frey (2010), "A robust question sets up subsequent instruction because it provides the information you need to further prompt, cue, or explain and model." Use prompts like the following to apply strong action verbs that will elicit a response from the student.

- "*Show* me your understanding of the success criteria."

- "*Describe* your understanding of the success criteria."

- "*Demonstrate* how you met that component of the success criteria."

- "*Teach* me the strategies you are using in meeting the success criteria."

This technique helps you "find out more about what students know, how they use information, and where any confusion may lie" (Fisher & Frey, 2010), rather than just asking the class as a whole if they have any questions. Prompting these verbal explanations plays an important role as well. According to *Education Week* assistant editor Sarah D. Sparks (2013), "Students who can verbally explain why they arrived at a particular answer have proved in prior studies to be more able to catch their own incorrect assumptions and generalize what they learn to other subjects." Giving students the opportunity to talk—to reach out to you—is valuable to student success. Professor Brenda Power (n.d.) explains, "The amount and quality of talk in classrooms is tied directly to student achievement." Therefore, a successful classroom is one where the teacher and the students are constantly reaching out to one another for understanding, analysis, and synthesis.

In addition, as you circulate throughout your classroom, consider the following questions, which take the focus off the student and instead centers it on the work.

- "Why did you choose that answer?"

- "Can you explain why you chose to use that particular strategy?"

- "Can you show me where you found that information?"

- "How do you know when you have run out of ways to answer this question?"

- "Based on your work so far, what strategy could you try next?"

By centering the questions on the work, you are, once again, demonstrating the importance and value of the process. Much like we discussed in the Encourage section in chapter 2 (page 49), the value of process praise and the importance of praising the work while not defining the student are critical.

If you find the student is able to *show* or *demonstrate* or *teach* a concept or component of the success criteria, then move on to the next student. However, if the student appears unsure about his or her work or shows you an example of his or her work that is incorrect, then you might need to apply the catch-and-release strategy. The catch-and-release strategy is helpful when the teacher has "noticed a pattern of confusion in several students" (Education World, 2017). Teachers briefly *catch* students and provide differentiated instruction to support their learning, and then *release* students back to their important work. The catches should be short, just a couple of minutes.

As an example, let's say the learning intention is about writing a summary paragraph based on a piece of text. Instead of a summary, the student has written a retelling. You notice that the student has included too many details in his or her paragraph, instead of adhering to the five Ws (who, what, where, when, and why) strategy that is necessary to complete the task.

Gently stop the work time, and quickly share a strategy or a resource that will benefit the entire class's learning process. Offer students a visual organizer to help them break down their thinking. As an example, offer students Janet Allen's (2008) graphic organizer, "Using the 5Ws and H to Find Information." This graphic organizer lists the five Ws on the left-hand side with a line next to each W on the right-hand side for students to write their responses. Spend a moment or two demonstrating how to find one of the five Ws, and then release students to practice with the rest. Those who need the five Ws graphic organizer can utilize it; those who do not need it can continue the method that works best for them.

Engagement Forms

Engagement forms offer students the chance to share their thinking but in written form. As opposed to questioning or miniconferences, some students prefer the writing process to communicate their thoughts; therefore, offering this brief form supports students who want to respond to the teacher's questions in a nonverbal way. Engagement forms are brief, much like the catch-and-release strategy, but in written form. It asks students to respond to the following three prompts.

1. List your progress on the success criteria so far.

2. Explain where you need assistance on a component of the success criteria.

3. Describe what doesn't make sense to you in the work we are doing.

About one-quarter or halfway through the class, after students have had time to work on the task, distribute these prompts on a printed-out form. Give students five minutes or fewer to complete the form. If you want students to have a choice between offering their thoughts verbally or via written feedback, you can even give them a choice in whether they complete the form at all. Next, collect the forms, and as you are circulating throughout the room, scan the responses. If you notice that several students left unsure or incomplete responses, gather those students together, and work with them in a small group. Or, if you see that several students need assistance for the same thing, you can interrupt the class for a catch-and-release opportunity. Do not make this form your exit ticket because then the conversation on how to assist the students has to wait until the next class. These prompts ask students to *do* something; they do not ask if the students understand what they are doing. The students have to respond by showing, in some way, their thinking.

Self-Assessment

As the lesson moves forward, give students some time to do a self-assessment, establishing their understanding of their work toward meeting the learning intention and success criteria. "When students self-assess, they internalize standards and assume greater responsibility for their own learning" (Moss & Brookhart, 2012, p. 15). In the first ten minutes of class, students had the opportunity to paraphrase the learning intention and success criteria during the ask component. Now, students can use the work they've done to review their paraphrased learning intention and success criteria to determine if they are meeting the success criteria.

This type of self-assessment is vital to student success and empowerment. Education professor James H. McMillan and research associate Jessica Hearn (2008) explain, "Self-assessment occurs when students judge their own work to improve performance as they identify discrepancies between current and desired performance" (p. 40).

Give students time during the lesson to check for their understanding and determine whether their understanding is realizing the performance they want. Consider creating a set of four self-assessment stations where students can choose a station and determine if they have indeed met the learning intention. For example, at one station, students could create pairs and talk through how they achieved the learning intention; at another station, students could work in collaborative groups and create questions to quiz each other to determine if they are on the right track; at the third station, students could write exit-ticket questions and ask another student to respond; and at the fourth station, students could write a brief journal entry about what they learned. You could even ask students how they want to self-assess their own understanding and use some of their suggestions as station activities.

Everette (2017) clarifies the usefulness of a process like this one: "Focused discussion and understanding of objectives can help students take ownership of their learning. That ownership is a key way to focus on mastery, no matter what the subject is." To help students apply that ownership, you might also give them a couple of minutes throughout the lesson when they can demonstrate examples of their work so far to you and to their peers. For example, you could set aside some space on the chalkboard designated for the specific task of showing one's work; or, if students have technology such as a tablet or laptop, they can share what they have learned on these devices; and finally, students can use mini-whiteboards to share their learning. Following are two examples of questions you can use to guide students' self-assessment both during and at the end of the lesson.

1. What specifically illustrates your understanding and synthesis of the learning intention?

2. What samples, models, or artifacts demonstrate your comprehension and application of the components of the success criteria?

You can provide these questions on a note card and collect them after the students have responded, or you can write these on a piece of poster paper and ask students to choose one and respond to it on a post-it note with students posting their notes next to the question on the poster paper. Finally, students can respond to another student as practice and, after receiving their peers' feedback, share their response with you.

Model

Because modeling allows students a means to self-assess ("Does my work align with the example I saw, or do I need to make improvements?"), it is an ideal method for providing students with guidance about the work they are to do (Catapano, n.d.). According to high school English teacher Jordan Catapano (n.d.):

> Models help students see what it is that they're supposed to produce. . . . When we combine the general explanation of a task with a concrete model of what their process or product should look like, we give students a direct image of their targeted outcome.

By using the model as a standard, students know the work that is expected, and they know how to modify the example to make their work more creative or more personalized. Models give students the consent to take their work to the next step. Teachers want students to use the model as a source of suggestions and possible inspiration. Therefore, models are opportunities for students to take a suggestion and make it their own.

Modeling also serves to improve the assignments teachers create. As a teacher, you will sometimes lose sight of what your assignments look like to a student, and creating work of your own requirements helps you sit in the student's chair for a few minutes and understand your task through that lens (Catapano, n.d.). Catapano (n.d.) further states:

> It's not uncommon to have to recalibrate or rethink our tasks once we do them for ourselves, so even the process of model creation can help us create more meaningful and coherent tasks. Plus, doing our own assignments can help validate our competence and expertise to students.

When students are unsure of how to proceed with an assigned task, models can help guide their work. When you notice students who are unsure of how to proceed, point back to the model you used, and work with them to see the relevance of the tasks you ask them to do. Catapano (n.d.) continues, "Modeling is an effective teaching strategy for almost any skill we may want our students to develop. . . . 'Showing' rather than just 'telling' students what to do will enhance their understanding." Beyond providing a road map for students' success, models also provide stimulating interactivity. According to Harbour et al. (2015), "Modeling is interactive . . . because it makes concepts accessible to the learners through structured, guided practice and reflecting learning and also because it increases on-task behavior" (as cited in Educational Research Newsletter & Webinars, 2015). Models present something students can interact with and utilize as an example of how to begin their project, or as an assurance that they are on the right track. Models offer students a kind of safety net that the work they are doing is indeed accurate.

As teachers are modeling a process, they are also instructing the process. Anita L. Archer and Charles A. Hughes (2011) explain that explicit instruction guides students "through the learning process with clear statements about the purpose and rationale for learning a new skill, clear expectations and demonstrations of the instructional target, and supported practice with feedback until independent mastery has been achieved" (p. 1). Specific modeling and explicit instruction will help students understand "how the individual tasks they're performing contribute to their growing set of skills and knowledge" (Catapano, n.d.).

Differentiation, tiering, and scaffolding are examples of *explicit instruction* teachers can use while modeling work for students. During a lesson, briefly interrupt students to show them the steps of the process again. Don't hesitate in presenting them the final product as well. Being aware of students' understanding during the lesson will enable you to make modifications on an as-needed basis so you ensure that each student achieves within his or her abilities. Throughout the course of the lesson, you will likely use differentiation, tiering, or scaffolding to help students succeed in reaching the learning intention and success criteria.

Note that these approaches, while having some similar concepts, do differ. In a differentiated classroom, a teacher will "provide specific alternatives for individuals to learn as deeply as possible and as quickly as possible, without assuming one student's road map for learning is identical to anyone else's" (Tomlinson, 2014, p. 4). In a tiered classroom, students receive instruction based on how challenging they find it to understand and achieve their learning intention and success criteria (Shapiro, n.d.). Finally, in a scaffolded classroom, the teacher builds in supports that enhance students' learning and help them in mastering tasks (IRIS Center, n.d.).

You will continually model during your lesson to ensure your students can master the learning intention and understand each success criterion. As Warren Haston (2007) explains in "Teacher Modeling as an Effective Teaching Strategy," students learn naturally when they have a model to imitate; therefore, applying differentiation, tiering, and scaffolding supports as you model your academic expectations will give your students various opportunities to meet the learning intention and ultimately be successful. In the following sections, I offer a quick primer on each of these instructional approaches.

Differentiating to Make a Difference

Differentiation allows the teacher to personalize instruction based on the needs of specific students or groups of students. According to the U.S. Department of Education's 2010 Education Technology Plan, *differentiation* "is instruction that is tailored to the learning preferences of different learners" (as cited in Bray & McClaskey, n.d.). Active planning and attention is the foundation of differentiation. Purposeful and meaningful lessons result from explicit planning and attention to students' needs and their abilities to be successful. By giving students the opportunity to ask and analyze, teachers can determine how to proceed using differentiated instruction to tailor their modeling for individual students or student groups based on the responses they observe or receive when posing questions as part of the ask component.

As an example, consider the following third-grade reading learning intention and success criteria from chapter 1 (page 18).

- **Third-grade reading:**

  - *Learning intention*—I can find and tell the main idea of the texts read in class and share examples with my peers.

  - *Success criteria*—I know I am successful because . . .

    1. I can ask questions about the text

    2. I can answer questions about the text

    3. I can use my questions and answers about the text to find the main idea

In this example, as the teacher plans the lesson, she has to pay special attention to the different rates at which students are achieving their success criteria and learning intention. Because she knows that several English learners in the class might need extra help in inquiry, she makes sure to plan to differentiate the lesson so all students can succeed. First, she creates small groups, where all students can practice their questioning skills with peers using the text. Then, she creates and laminates a series of question starters for each small group (including those for whom English is their primary language) that will assist the English learners in generating questions about the text. Initially, the teacher encourages students to ask questions without the use of the question starters, but if students feel they need extra help, she encourages them to use the question starters. In differentiating the lesson, the teacher ensures that all students remain part of the lesson. Those small groups that need the question starters accomplish that part of the success criteria. Those that don't need the question starters use them as validation for the original questions they create.

Then, when the students are ready to answer questions about the text, give them the opportunity to answer those questions in writing or by sharing their responses with another student. If students have written their responses, encourage them to find a partner to read and review their responses, encouraging feedback and conversation. For the students who have preferred to talk through their responses, ask them to find a partner to listen to their responses and jot down the key points; then, discuss if those key points need further expansion. Finally, consider giving students the option of working in pairs, in small groups, or individually to use their questions and answers to find the main idea of the text.

Carol Ann Tomlinson (2014) says, "Teachers who differentiate provide specific alternatives for individuals to learn as deeply as possible and as quickly as possible, without assuming one student's road map for learning is identical to anyone else's" (p. 4). This lesson gives all students the chance to learn how to ask questions, and it also provides a road map for those who need a little extra help on their journey.

Tiering to Teach

Education writer Janelle Cox (n.d.a) explains, "Tiered assignments do not lock students into ability boxes. Instead, particular student clusters are assigned specific tasks within each group according to their readiness and comprehension—without making them feel completely compartmentalized away from peers at different achievement levels." Tiering content (not to be confused with the tiered response to intervention; Buffum, Mattos, & Malone, 2018) helps students take the learning apart and focus on one piece of learning at a time. Through tiering, teachers can determine how many tiers are necessary based on a student's need. For example, in "Differentiated Instruction Strategies: Tiered Assignments," Cox (n.d.a) introduces six ways to structure tier assignments that "reach all learners and accommodate each student's learning style." As a result of tiering, teachers have the flexibility to create opportunities for student growth, and students have choices in how they demonstrate what they know and are able to do.

Tiered assignments allow teachers to vary a student's work by adjusting a task's complexity, depth, and abstractness based on the student's current ability level (EL Education, n.d.a). Therefore, there is no set number of recommended tiers; rather, the teacher has the flexibility to determine what students need based on the needs of the assignment. As an example, consider the following sixth- to eighth-grade science and technical subjects learning intention and success criteria from chapter 1 (page 19).

- **Sixth- to eighth-grade science and technical subjects:**
  - *Learning intention*—I can learn the differences among superstition, pseudoscience, and science.
  - *Success criteria*—I know I am successful because . . .
    1. I can define *superstition*, *pseudoscience*, and *science*
    2. I can demonstrate the differences using a graphic organizer
    3. I can find real-life examples of superstition, pseudoscience, and science and share them with the class

To tier this assignment, the teacher creates groups of students organized by their current ability with the learning intention. First, she puts students in like clusters based on their readiness and comprehension. Next, she determines that all students will define the terms, but one group will be responsible for specifically finding synonyms for the words *superstition*, *pseudoscience*, and *science*. This particular cluster will focus on word meaning since this group is ready and able to comprehend the first success criterion. In addition, when these students finish the definitions and synonyms, they will share them with the class so other students benefit from their vocabulary work. In this way, the teacher tiers the work for specific groups of students. When one group shares its vocabulary learning, they give students another way to make meaning. Of course, the teacher could create other tiers for groups depending on what type of ability development those students needed.

Scaffolding to Optimize Success

When teachers scaffold instruction, they typically break up a learning experience. As you have likely surmised, the development of learning intentions, success criteria, and learning progressions are themselves examples of scaffolding instruction. In the case of the modeling component of FRAME during class instruction, scaffolding instruction offers the teacher numerous opportunities to model each learning intention and success criteria *for students*, so they have the opportunity to reflect on each part of the process. Cox (n.d.b) explains:

> Scaffolding is . . . a structure that allows students to gradually reach higher levels of understanding. . . . The teacher's job is to build upon each student's experience and knowledge as they learn. They can do this by modeling and having students practice. Effective teachers usually find that it is easier to start by teaching students a new strategy when the content is familiar to them. Then, over time, the teacher can present new content that is less familiar to the students so that they [sic] students can apply what they have learned previously.

Give students a chance to share their understanding with you. You can do this in a variety of ways, using strategies we established for the ask component: have one-to-one miniconferences as you circulate throughout the classroom, share a brief engagement feedback form that small groups use to gather group success, prompt whole-class structured questioning, or simply ask students to explain how they have met the learning intention. As an example, if a student is finding a short story challenging, during a miniconference, offer pictures that show the setting, characters, and events to help him or her make meaning.

Whatever method you decide to use, gather feedback more than once throughout the lesson. Do not wait until the end of the lesson to determine student readiness to move on. Do not rely on the standard thumbs-up, thumbs-down, or thumbs-sideways approach. Do not ask your students if they "get it." Chances are your students will say "yes" just to move on, regardless of whether they understand it.

Encourage

Teachers often hear students say things like, "I'm not good at . . ." and settle on that phrase as explaining their inability to conquer a formula, solve a problem, or analyze a soliloquy. As a student, I said, "I'm just not good at math," so often and failed so often that I wholeheartedly believed what I said. Then, in my senior year of college, I learned I had to take a mathematics class to graduate. In truth, when I took the class, I didn't find it difficult at all. As a matter of fact, I loved the class, but not because I was older and more tolerant of mathematics. I loved it because the teacher explained and demonstrated the mathematics and encouraged all of us to be successful mathematics students. She enthusiastically believed that all of us could be mathematicians and love and use mathematics in our everyday lives.

That is how learning should be—passionately believing that you can and your students can. This, as we covered in chapter 2 (page 49), requires a growth mindset. In this section, we'll take those ideas and expand them to fit your approach for a full class as opposed to those first ten minutes.

Perhaps surprisingly, praise can be just as problematic to the growth mindset as negative self-talk is. From participation ribbons to perfect-attendance certificates, many students are used to "earning" awards and praise at every corner. However, to encourage a growth mindset, it's important to move away from praising students and instead offer your students challenging opportunities to show you what they know (Dweck, 2006).

It's not unusual to hear teachers say to a student, "Oh, you're so smart!" or "That must come easy for you." However, these phrases, according to *The Atlantic* writer James Hamblin (2015), help "develop the idea that they are smart, [which means] they also tend to develop vulnerability around relinquishing that label." When students hear these types of comments over and over again, it becomes counterproductive. They develop a fear of failure that prevents them from challenging themselves to tackle more complex concepts. When classwork becomes challenging or problematic, those "smart" students are more likely to give up. Often, students haven't had the experiences necessary to build perseverance because they've never attempted work that caused them productive struggle. Jensen (2019) believes this willingness to persevere is an essential trait for students to develop what he calls an "achievement mindset," a belief in one's self to overcome obstacles and master challenging learning objectives. When students lack this mindset, it leads them to conclude that if they can't solve the problem, they must not be so smart, after all. They are missing the idea that they can grow their knowledge, skills, and intellect.

During class, you want to give your students challenging opportunities to show you and their peers what they know. And, when they do get stuck, Hamblin (2015) encourages teachers to emphasize enhancing performance. He explains:

> What matters for improving performance is that a person is challenged, which requires a mindset that is receptive to being challenged—if not actively seeking out challenge and failure. And that may be the most important thing a teacher can impart. (Hamblin, 2015)

Therefore, keep the encouragement coming, but refrain from praising the student, and instead encourage the efforts, strategies, and ideas the student applies to solve the problem. Let students know that you have chosen work that is designed especially for them—challenging work that will require reflection from creative, inquisitive, global citizens like themselves.

As you move throughout your classroom, observing student work and checking for understanding, encourage your students to do their best work. Let them know you trust their ability to be tenacious learners. Again, don't offer praise just for the sake of praise. Empty praise doesn't mean anything. And praise should center not on the work but on the student's ability to use various processes and strategies to do the work. You need to encourage the learner and encourage the work. As students make progress and begin to achieve, connect that progress to the effort they put in. This takes the lens off the student and instead focuses on the process, resources, and strategies the student used to help him or her solve the problem, fix the error, or simply think through a difficult situation. Applying these strategies gives the student a chance to reprocess instead of him or her shutting down due to the frustration of being "wrong." Instead, the student is encouraged to look at the process and try again. Collectively, these things instill in students a growth mindset because the focus is on the process and not necessarily the product. The teacher is encouraging the student to review the strategies or the work and not label the learner. The teacher wants the student to realize that as he or she keeps working forward, he or she is open to new ways of trying and new ways of doing. In short, students are developing a growth mindset. Here are some helpful phrases aimed at checking for understanding.

- "Let's look at the strategies you've used and decide if we should try another one."

- "Rereading the text is a worthwhile strategy. As you reread, what new information did you find?"

- "Let's look at your work; explain how you decided to try that formula."

Asking students to explain their work helps them determine if they are on the right track. How often have you yourself recognized a flaw in your explanation of something only as you're saying it aloud? As they explain their work to you, praise the process and their motivation to stick with it. When you give students the opportunity to explain their learning process to you, they will truly be in charge of their own thinking and their own learning. By taking charge of one's own thinking and one's own learning, students begin to trust themselves to solve problems instead of relying on the teacher for the next step. Students become encouraged and empowered by their own ability to move forward in the process, instead of depending on someone else to get them there.

Let students know you expect they will stay with the work and not give up because the work is focused on mastery within each student's individual ability to meet the success criteria, which are themselves composed of scaffolded learning progressions. This is why both are numbered so that the gradual acquisition of skills is clear. If a student is unable to master a success criterion, the teacher and student will confer to determine what learning progressions the student needs to master and move on. If the teacher observes a group of students unable to meet a specific success criterion, then the teacher can re-examine the learning progressions to differentiate, tier, or further scaffold them to meet the needs of those particular students. Encouragement through this process can take many different forms—an inspiring word, a gentle nod, or a listening ear—and is meant to assist students in determining the best process for their work, not necessarily focusing on their intellect within the work. Therefore, encouragement offers opportunities for ruminating, revising, and reflecting toward students developing a sense of their academic selves. Applying a growth mindset helps students move beyond product and focus on the pieces of the process.

In addition to a growth mindset, teachers should encourage a *benefit mindset*; this mindset supports an academic family by urging students to build and apply skills and knowledge in productive and supportive ways. The benefit mindset is a natural extension of the growth mindset. According to educator Robert Ward (2018a), this mindset "takes the strong seeds of self-belief and self-improvement that growth mindset sows and brings them to fruition in ways that enhance not only one's own life but the lives of others as well."

For example, a benefit mindset is valuable in the classroom because it helps students review each other's work and provide feedback in a nonjudgmental way. If you ask your students to review their classmates' work without explicitly teaching these skills, oftentimes they will read it and return it with a simple *Good job* written at the top. Teachers can positively influence the art of collaboration, along with sensitive evaluation and critique, when they teach it through a benefit mindset lens. Ward (2018a) continues, "Feelings of community and collaboration make learning meaningful for all, and this sense of shared significance is at the heart" of the benefit mindset.

You can inspire a benefit mindset in your classroom by making students aware of the language they use when collaborating. Offer students a list of phrases they could use when peer reviewing or evaluating or critiquing any idea or suggestion. Ward (2018c) advises using phrases such as the following.

- _____ is meaningful because _____.
- _____ is memorable because _____.
- Avoid _____ so that _____.
- Consider changing _____ in order to _____.
- Perhaps move a level deeper by _____.
- Try making your ideas more personal by _____. (pp. 72–75)

These sentence starters offer students opportunities to employ specific language that supports making collaboration meaningful for all. In addition, this brief example of inspiring the benefit mindset helps illustrate the value of the process of the work and the need to encourage students to share their efforts, strategies, and ideas toward improvement and, ultimately, success.

The Exemplary Classroom

The exemplary classroom scenario for this chapter reflects an observation I conducted of a sophomore geometry class at my school. The teacher, Mr. Moore, first *focused* his intentions on a classroom exercise to help students self-reflect on their work on a recent test. He decided to create a series of expert stations where students could review their test results, identify areas of struggle, and work to revise in these areas by working with other students who were successful in these areas. Each station, which consisted of a pod of six desks pushed together, was dedicated to a specific test question that proved challenging for students. Before class began, Mr. Moore stood outside of his classroom, *reaching* out to each student with an enthusiastic "Good morning" and excitedly telling each student that today was "Test review day! Yeah!"

After the bell rang and during the first ten minutes of class, Mr. Moore introduced the FRAME model, applying the learning intention and success criteria that he had written on the whiteboard the day before. The whiteboard was always located in the front of the room where students could see it. He read to students the learning intention and success criteria.

- **Learning intention:** I can make sense of problems and persevere in solving them.

- **Success criteria:** I know I am successful because—

    1. I can collaborate with my peers and explain to myself and to them why I solved a problem the way I did and, if my answer is incorrect, look for other ways to solve it

    2. I can check my answers with my peers

    3. I can check my peers' answers to the problems I got wrong and try different methods

    4. I can ask myself and my peers, "Does this answer make sense?"

    5. I can successfully solve the incorrect problems

Next, Mr. Moore directed his students to sit in their peer pods, preassigned small groups where students sit upon first entering the classroom. Once students sat down, Mr. Moore asked them to greet their classmates and *focus* their attention on the learning intention and success criteria. (Notice how the focus component becomes a recurring part of using FRAME.) He explained that he set aside the entire class period for student review, questions, and revisions. He asked each peer pod to read the learning intention and success criteria. This gave students a chance to prepare themselves for the new learning ahead. Then, he *asked* each group to paraphrase the learning intention and success criteria. The room began to buzz as students read the learning intention and success criteria again in their small groups. Many students commented that they wanted to see the problems they had gotten wrong and were looking forward to the opportunity to correct them.

Mr. Moore asked for two student volunteers to explain what the task was for that day, which two students did, using their own words. Then, Mr. Moore asked students to stand up and move their desks to create six stations of six desks each. After students had created their stations, he explained that he would be directing them where to sit and that each station would include three student volunteers who had solved the problem correctly and three students who didn't. He *modeled* to students that the student volunteers would be the experts and the other three students would be working with the experts to see what they had done wrong on that particular problem. The experts would explain their methods of solving the problem, and the other students would review and revise their incorrect answer.

Then, Mr. Moore *encouraged* the use of the phrase, "Does this make sense?" when reflecting on the problem. In using that phrase, or language similar to it, he explained that the students were thinking about the steps necessary to solve the problem and perhaps realizing where they had made their error (if they had made one). He also encouraged students to ask questions of the experts at their station since the expert students might have used different methods to solve the problem. Next, Mr. Moore walked throughout the room, handing back their tests. He reached out to each student, directing the students where to sit, making sure that at each cluster of desks were three expert students and three students that needed assistance; in addition, he encouraged students to grab a pencil and protractor from the supplies bin if they needed one.

Each station had a different problem that proved challenging for some students. Mr. Moore asked the mathematics experts to share with the class the problem they were going to demonstrate. As an example, at the first expert station, three students explained they were going to demonstrate how they solved problem number 2. At the second expert station, three students said they were going to demonstrate how they solved problem number 5, and so on. Mr. Moore had successfully implemented the FRAME model, and his class was ready for the learning he had designed.

During the lesson, Mr. Moore enhanced students' *focus* by repeating the FRAME components once again as he walked throughout the classroom. He connected with (*reached*) his students by bending down at each station and listening to their explanations, questions, and clarifications. He stopped at various stations and asked students to clarify their thinking in how they had originally solved the problem and identify what new learning they now had.

Several students asked Mr. Moore to help them understand a problem. When he asked why they weren't asking the experts, the students commented that they were still having trouble and needed more clarification. At that point, he did a quick catch and release. He *asked* how many other students had difficulty solving that particular problem. Many more hands went up. Mr. Moore went to the SMART Board and *modeled* to students how to solve it but then encouraged students to find other ways to solve the problem. He released them to discuss. After several minutes, he caught them again with a similar problem he had written on the board, and he asked the entire class to solve it.

After several more minutes, Mr. Moore stopped class again and again focused students back to the success criteria. He asked them to silently think about the paraphrased success criteria their group had discussed. Had they met the steps? Were they stuck on a particular step? He *encouraged* students to self-assess their time and to determine what they still needed to do. Again, Mr. Moore walked around the room, stopping at various stations and asking students to explain how they solved the problems; in addition, he called various students to the side chalkboard who, upon his observation, needed extra support and worked individually with them on some challenging skills.

Near the end of the block, Mr. Moore asked students to thank their peers and share one or two positive, encouraging experiences from this collaboration. Several students commented on how they liked working with their peers on solving the problem or how they liked having their peers show them more than one way to come to the answer. Mr. Moore's class often works in groups, and he often shows his students more than one way to solve a problem. However, it appeared as though students felt more successful from these expert stations. Mr. Moore asked students to move back to their original seats and asked them to hand in their revised tests. He thanked the class for their hard work and lauded the value of working with one's peers in achieving the answer.

Implementing FRAME within the classroom creates a focused, collaborative community where students in all grade levels and with all abilities engage in important work that encourages productive struggle, critical-thinking skills, and self-management.

Conclusion

Teachers should embed FRAME within a lesson seamlessly but purposefully. Utilizing each component of FRAME gives students the routine they long for within their sometimes-chaotic school day. Communicating objectives that offer opportunities for growth gives students the motivation they need to know that they will be successful by the end of the lesson. Intentional eye contact, relevant conversation, and correct pronunciation of students' names convey to them they are part of a classroom community—a community that doesn't end at the end of the school day. Continuing to ask questions and analyze the day's work gives students purpose and shows them how to make worthwhile connections among the various topics they explore during the typical school day. Most important, however, is continuing to encourage the valuable learning students do. Students need to know that their tenacity and willingness to recall, understand, apply, analyze, evaluate, and create illustrate their genuine desire for discovery, growth, and achievement.

Do-Now Suggestions for Your Classroom or Collaborative Team

Reflect on the following suggestions and questions in collaborative teams or as individual teachers to support your work and conversations around implementing the FRAME model.

- Give examples of how you refer to the learning intention and success criteria during a lesson.

- Explain your methods for ensuring students understand and apply the learning intention and success criteria.

- Identify ways in which you reach out to each student during a lesson. How does reaching out prompt engagement and motivation?

- Choose one clarifying question and one probing question to use in your class tomorrow. How do these questions help further establish a connection to your students?

- How could you embed one-to-one conferences in your classroom?

- How might you modify an engagement form for your students so that it suits their current ability levels?

- Describe one way you do each of the following: differentiate to make a difference, tier to teach, and scaffold to optimize success. Offer concrete examples to share with your colleagues.

- How can you use self-assessment to support all students of all abilities?

- Create a T-chart of the positives and negatives associated with encouraging meaningful feedback. Apply a positive feedback strategy to your practice in your next class. Does it successfully impact the learning environment; if so, how?

- Identify explicit ways educators can create a genuine desire for discovery, growth, and achievement among students.

CHAPTER 4

How to Use FRAME for Peer Observation and Feedback Among Teachers

All teachers close their classroom door at one time or another for a variety of reasons, from limiting disruptions (student chatter in the hallways) to concealing a lack of confidence (thoughts like, *What happens if someone is a better teacher than I am?*). The closed-door approach is certainly acceptable in some instances. But what happens when closing classroom doors, literally and metaphorically, becomes the norm for a school? What happens when teachers, as education specialists Jeffrey Mirel and Simona Goldin (2012) state, "take leave of one another, walk to their classrooms to meet their students, and close the door"?

Teaching and learning cannot occur in isolation. Teaching is, according to Parker J. Palmer (2007), "essentially communal" (p. 118), a "connectedness" (p. 118) that all teachers innately need to support their students. Therefore, if teachers are indeed centered on creating an academic family for students, teachers must begin by learning from each other in a risk-free, nonjudgmental way.

At this point, you have done the heavy lifting of learning the FRAME structure. You understand the acronym, the meaning of its components, and their purpose. You have the knowledge to implement FRAME during the first ten minutes of your class and know how to continue applying it throughout a lesson. But the opportunity to apply FRAME doesn't have to stop there. In this last chapter, you will explore how to utilize FRAME, through a structured series of guiding questions, as an informal teacher-observation tool to help support each other and enhance teacher efficacy and effectiveness. This chapter ends with a final example of FRAME's use in an exemplary classroom and a series of do-now suggestions for your classroom or collaborative team.

Key Aspects of Using FRAME for Peer Observation

Unlike previous chapters, I do not break down this process by the FRAME components but rather by the key aspects of successfully engaging in this collaborative work. These aspects include the importance of establishing an open-door policy with colleagues, how you prepare students for the presence of other teachers in the classroom, and the steps you should take before conducting the observation. Only after establishing these key criteria are you ready to implement FRAME as a peer-observation and feedback tool.

Open-Door Policy

The work of using FRAME for peer observation begins even before your first discussions with a colleague. Begin by creating an atmosphere of collegiality; let teachers know they are welcome in your classroom. What makes a classroom inviting to a fellow teacher? According to Sarah Moore, a ninth-grade Spanish teacher, it's the "personal touches like handwritten posters and pictures, student work, flexible seating, an open door and a smiling teacher" (personal communication, August 18, 2019). But start small, especially if you have some anxiety about your fellow educators watching you. Matthew O. Richardson (2000) explains, "Most teachers are uneasy when anyone besides their own students watch [sic] them teach" (p. 10). To ease this anxiety, perhaps first share a lesson idea with a department member or a fellow educator. For example, ask the teacher across the hall if he or she would be interested in designing a cross-curricular lesson or whether he or she would be willing to brainstorm some ideas. Explain to your colleague that you are trying a new strategy and invite him or her to watch you teach it. Or, you could mention to the teacher down the hall that his or her class always seems to be filled with laughter and ask whether you could observe a lesson sometime. Don't hesitate to ask a teacher to stop in and be a part of your classroom experience. Then, offer an invitation to come in and see the lesson. Gonzalez (2013) explains, "You can have an open-door policy and still have a closed classroom door: Just let your peers know when they are welcome."

Student Mind Shift

As you move toward extending an invitation to have a colleague observe your classroom instruction, it's important to similarly prepare your students. The first week of school is the perfect time to let your students know that fellow teachers may be coming into the classroom to observe your teaching. If you miss your window during that first week, that's OK. You can talk to your students about this at any point during the year, so long as they have sufficient notice and understanding that an observation may occur during the grading period. Regardless of the timing, what is important is that you get your students comfortable with the idea of having guests in the classroom. You want them to know that their classroom is a place of learning for *everyone*—not just the students, but teachers too. Explain to your students that, just like them, for teachers to become better teachers, it's imperative that they practice, and they come to their colleagues' classrooms to observe and learn.

As part of this discussion with your students, explain to them that you also want to become a better teacher and that means you welcome feedback from your peers—much like students do when they work in small groups, asking for assistance from their peers. Conducting this discussion helps students understand that the observer isn't just there to watch the teacher, but also themselves. Richardson (2000) explains:

> Students . . . almost always react the same way when they notice a "visitor" in their classroom. They immediately believe that "someone is checking the teacher out." It never occurs to them that the visitor may actually be "checking them out," or, even more importantly, there to learn from a colleague. (pp. 11–12)

As part of this process, give students the opportunity to ask questions about classroom guests. What do they want to know more about? Are they uncomfortable about visitors in the classroom? If so, ask why that is and what you can do to alleviate their anxiety. Explain that when a guest visits, it is not necessary to show off or become the class comedian. Rather, encourage students to be themselves and focus on being the students that you are proud of. Explain that guests offer the opportunity for growth and for preparing a better teacher—for them.

Peer Observation Preparation

Once you and the observer agree on a date, it's time to prepare. Educator Tricia Bracher (2014), writing for *The Guardian*, advises that teachers make copies of lesson plans and any other applicable resources to share with the observer, as well as any support staff that may be present. I am less strict on this and believe what resources you share depends on your comfort level with your materials and with your colleague; however, the idea of sharing your work helps reinforce your open-door policy and certainly creates a collaborative atmosphere of listening and learning.

Implementation of FRAME for Teachers' Peer Observation and Feedback

One aspect of classroom observations that often creates stress for the teacher being observed is that such observation typically comes from the top down; that is, they are administration driven. Whether it's a walkthrough to gather a snapshot of one's teaching or a bona fide teacher evaluation, a traditional teacher observation carried out by administrators can be a nerve-racking experience for the observed teacher. This dynamic can make *any* observation activity feel stressful, but ASCD faculty member Jason Flom (2014) explains why bottom-up observations can reduce or eliminate such anxiety:

> Teachers are more likely to fully embrace the opportunities afforded by peer-to-peer observations when they have played a role in identifying the essential questions to be investigated and observed—that is, when a bottom-up approach is used. Administrators need to find ways to give teachers an authentic voice when developing the questions that matter to them, their students, and their practice.

Emily Dolci Grimm, Trent Kaufman, and Dave Doty (2014) clarify the benefits of teacher-driven observation as compared to a top-down approach:

> Teacher-driven observation addresses these problems by empowering teachers with a classroom-embedded process to refine their instruction. Through teacher-driven observation, teachers engage peers in gathering and analyzing classroom data—data that speak to the unique context of their own classrooms. This approach has demonstrated potential to meaningfully improve instruction and student achievement.

That empowerment is extremely beneficial since teachers can refine their instruction based on what they determine is a need in *their* classroom. This is also where the components of FRAME can be of tremendous service to both the observer and the teacher he or she is observing. For this purpose, I developed the "FRAME Peer Observation and Feedback Form for Teachers" (figure 4.1, pages 86–87), which encourages teachers to use FRAME methodology to intimately look at all aspects of their teaching—not just the content or how they deliver it in general, but rather the way in which they provide it to all students of all abilities. (You will find a reproducible version of this figure in the appendix, pages 105–107.)

There are many scenarios in which you can use this form to gain valuable observation feedback. For example, you could independently ask a colleague to informally observe a lesson, perhaps one that is new or one that you have revised; you could share the form with your collaborative team and then use it for structured, planned peer evaluations; or you could simply ask a colleague to review you prior to a more formal administrator-driven evaluative review.

Once you have set the groundwork for the peer observations, share the peer observation and feedback form as a way to gather information on your teaching. If your colleague is unfamiliar with FRAME, set aside time to discuss its components and how its structure within this form enables teachers to focus on what they deem important to their practice. You can also adapt this form as much as you wish to make it your own. For example, if a teacher wants feedback on the types of questions she is asking—Are they basic recall or higher-order-thinking questions?—she can focus on the Ask area of the observation form. Because of the specificity the form affords, the teacher is more likely to be invested in this type of feedback opportunity than if a supervisor vaguely told her she needed to work on her questioning skills.

For this reason, the idea of observing each other and collecting data for improvement is not tied to an evaluation; rather, it's a way to become better instructors for the sake of your students. Robert J. Marzano (2011) explains that "observing teachers identifying instructional practices they'll continue to use because they saw other teachers employing them effectively" (p. 81) assists teachers in bringing new ideas and strategies to their classroom—ideas and strategies that they know are successful because they observed them within an authentic classroom experience. Graham D. Hendry and Gary R. Oliver of the University of Sydney (2012) explain, "In other words, watching someone teach well inspires us to try the strategy, and when we too are successful, our belief in the usefulness of what we saw and what we are capable of is enhanced."

Guiding Questions	Observations and Feedback
Focus • Were the learning intention and success criteria clearly visible to all students? • Were the learning intention and success criteria written in student-friendly language? • Did the teacher establish the learning intention and success criteria with the students? If so, how? • How did the teacher know if the students knew and understood today's expectations? What evidence did the teacher have to support that belief?	
Reach • Did the teacher offer a greeting to each student? If so, what type (verbal greeting, handshake, brief conversation)? • How did students respond to the teacher? Did they appear to feel welcome and comfortable, or did they show reluctance or anxiety? • Is there something else the teacher could do to demonstrate a classroom community?	
Ask • Did the teacher return to the learning intention and success criteria to ensure students' understanding? • How did students engage with the learning intention and success criteria? Did they ask questions? Could they successfully paraphrase the learning intention and success criteria? What evidence shows their engagement? • What could the teacher have done to engage students who appeared uninterested in the lesson? • How did the teacher create opportunities for all students to show they were engaged? • Did the teacher check for understanding? If so, what checks did the teacher use to determine if the students understood the learning intention and success criteria? • What could the teacher do for students whose understanding is unclear?	

Model

- Did the teacher show the students what to do or tell them what to do?
- Explain how the teacher showed students how to achieve the success criteria.
- What differentiation dynamics did the teacher use to ensure he or she was doing the following?
  - Meeting individual learning styles
  - Grouping students by shared interest, topic, or ability
  - Assessing students' learning using a variety of formative assessments
  - Managing the classroom to create a safe and supportive environment
  - Continually adjusting content to meet student needs
- What tiering techniques did the teacher use to ensure he or she was doing the following?
  - Developing varying levels of complexity of the task
  - Offering various degrees of direction for students needing additional support
  - Creating opportunities for equity among student work
- What scaffolding systems did the teacher use to ensure he or she was doing the following?
  - Building on the prior knowledge a learner has of a particular topic
  - Creating opportunities for peer collaboration and learning
  - Designing an environment where students are free to ask questions and challenge thinking in a respectful, culturally sensitive way

Encourage

- How did the teacher encourage students to participate? Was the encouragement focused on fostering a growth mindset, or did it focus on offering praise?
- Did students encourage each other? If so, how? If not, why not?
- What was the teacher's final suggestion or comment to students that promotes an encouraging attitude?

Final Thoughts

Figure 4.1: FRAME peer observation and feedback form for teachers.

While the form lists guiding questions that apply the entire FRAME acronym, it is impossible to take observational notes on all the guiding questions simply because it is too much information to cover in one class. Attempting to observe the entire structure will take away from the necessary focus the observer needs when providing valuable, targeted feedback. Before the scheduled observation date, meet with your observer to decide what you specifically want feedback on, such as your implementation of a specific element of FRAME. Whatever you and your observer decide, gather notes and anecdotal data on those questions only. In that way, the notes will be thorough and detailed. If you want to use the full form, instead plan for multiple observations in which the observer is focusing on just one or two aspects of the FRAME components at a time.

The observer can gather data in a variety of ways, such as the following.

- Writing what the teacher said or what the teacher did in the appropriate box

- Answering the questions based on what the observer saw or heard

- Gathering examples based on what the observer saw or heard

- Asking more guiding questions based on the classroom observation

After data are gathered, the teacher and the observer should meet to unpack the findings. According to Marilyn Chu (2012), the observer can "begin by asking open-ended questions about a teacher's work" (p. 22). These open-ended questions help the teacher in thinking deeply about his or her practice. Chu (2012) goes on to explain the importance of having a safe climate for adult learning; that is, a climate in which colleagues listen with interest, respect, and empathy. This kind of safe climate supports the teacher in sharing his or her teaching philosophy, goals, visions, and ideas. In addition, while citing Daniel R. Schienfeld, Karen M. Haigh, and Sandra J. P. Schienfeld (2008), Chu (2012) comments that:

> Scaffolding teachers' development with stimulating questions, careful observation, and emphasizing thinking deeply requires "promot(ing) experiences and types of development in the teachers that enable and motivate them to promote similar experiences and types of development in the children." (p. 23)

Because it is all part of a teacher-driven process, the discussion is low risk for the teacher and therefore creates reflective dialogue meant to hone a teacher's practice. Begin by revisiting the goal of the observation in the first place: Is it to gain feedback on a new or improved lesson? Is the goal to have an opportunity for collaborative teams to gain feedback from peer evaluations? Or, is the goal to have a practice round for an upcoming administrative evaluation?

Always keep that goal in mind when sharing the successes and challenges of the lesson because, much like revisiting the learning intention and success criteria in the classroom with his or her students, revisiting the goal of this observation keeps the teacher and observer focused on what the conversation should be about and helps to maintain a professional atmosphere in regard to the process rather than on labeling the teacher or labeling his or her gaps in teaching.

The Exemplary Classroom

For this final exemplary classroom, you will see an example of how to apply FRAME as a teacher-efficacy tool by utilizing a structured series of guiding questions to help colleagues support each other and enhance their teaching.

Ms. Smith, our seventh-grade English teacher, designed a lesson focusing on citing textual evidence to support inferences and why inferences are important. For this lesson, she used Ray Bradbury's (1998) short story, "All Summer in a Day." She asked me if I would apply FRAME to observe her lesson and provide feedback. She wanted to make sure she was following the protocol during the first ten minutes of her class and then embedding it successfully throughout her lesson. I gave her a copy of the "FRAME Peer Observation and Feedback Form for Teachers" featured in figure 4.1 (pages 86–87) and explained that I would not be able to take notes on each concept within FRAME from a single observation. I asked if there were specific components she wanted me to focus on, and she explained she wanted to hone her differentiation skills.

When you observe a colleague using FRAME, determine specifically what the teacher wants you to observe. Make sure your task is clear. Does he or she want to determine how well he or she has applied FRAME only during the first ten minutes of class? Does he or she want you to concentrate specifically on a FRAME component, such as modeling, during the lesson? As the observer, tailor your focus to what your colleague needs. Also, you can take all of your observational notes on one "FRAME for Peer Observation and Feedback Form for Teachers" tool, if that is easier for you, or you can use separate copies for the first ten minutes and for the full lesson.

Because Ms. Smith wanted feedback on the first ten minutes *and* on how she embedded FRAME throughout the rest of the class, I decided to make two copies of the "FRAME Peer Observation and Feedback Form for Teachers," so I could keep my notes separate for both phases of the class. For me, it was easier to make two copies of the blank form and keep my notes separated. Because Ms. Smith had also asked me to focus on differentiation skills, I deleted the scaffolding and tiering examples from the modeling section of the feedback tool and concentrated on differentiation.

First, we set up a date when I could observe her lesson on using inference to support analysis. I requested a copy of the short story she was using so I could review it ahead of time. In addition, I also asked her to send me her learning intention and success criteria before the lesson. I reviewed the story prior to my observation, made notations about inference, and read her learning intention and success criteria for the short story. Note that these actions all factored into my observation of the focus component of FRAME.

Figure 4.2 (pages 91–93) features my notes using the "FRAME Peer Observation and Feedback Form for Teachers" for the first ten minutes of Ms. Smith's class. Notice that I commented on some of the guiding questions explicitly, while other questions I used as a guideline. In addition, I kept track of the time Ms. Smith used for each FRAME component during the first ten minutes. It was important to Ms. Smith to stay within the ten-minute guideline so students had enough time for the remainder of the lesson.

Upon completing her use of FRAME in the first ten minutes of class, Ms. Smith immediately transitioned into the day's lesson. After encouraging her students to ask questions, she distributed the short story. Next, she asked students to make groups of three. Once students were in their groups, she began to embed FRAME within the lesson. Figure 4.3 (pages 94–96) shows my notes in the feedback tool for the remaining thirty-five-minute class period.

After class ended, I thanked her for giving me the opportunity to observe her and her students, and we decided to meet in two days to discuss the lesson. That afternoon, I made a copy of each of the forms and gave them to her. I encouraged her to read and annotate my notes so we could discuss when we met.

Ms. Smith and I met in the English office. Once again, I thanked her for the chance to watch her teach. I had both of the forms with notes to discuss, and she had the copies I had given her. We then proceeded to break down her instruction through the lens of each FRAME component.

Even though I separated the observation—applying FRAME during the first ten minutes of class and her work embedding FRAME throughout the lesson—we chose to discuss the class as a whole. As a result, we looked at both sets of notes and discussed them together. The following sections detail our discussion through the lens of each FRAME component.

Guiding Questions	Observations and Feedback
Focus • Were the learning intention and success criteria clearly visible to all students? • Were the learning intention and success criteria written in student-friendly language? • Did the teacher establish the learning target and success criteria with the students? If so, how? • How did the teacher know if the students knew and understood today's expectations? What evidence did the teacher have to support that belief?	*(The day before)* *Yes, the learning intention and success criteria are located on an easel in the front of the room and are written in student-friendly language.* *Learning intention: I can correctly cite evidence from a short story to show how inferences support analysis.* *Success criteria: I know I am successful because I can—* *1. Correctly cite evidence from the text.* *2. Connect the evidence to support the inference.* *3. Apply the inference to support the analysis.* *Ms. Smith read the learning intention and success criteria out loud to students.*
Reach • Did the teacher offer a greeting to each student? If so, what type (verbal greeting, handshake, brief conversation)? • How did students respond to the teacher? Did they appear to feel welcome and comfortable, or did they show reluctance or anxiety? • Is there something else the teacher could do to demonstrate a classroom community?	*(Before the bell rang)* *Ms. Smith stood outside her classroom and verbally greeted each individual student, using their names, while also taking attendance. She also offered a whole-class greeting.*

Figure 4.2: FRAME peer observation and feedback form for teachers—implementing FRAME during the first ten minutes of class.

Continued ▶

Guiding Questions	Observations and Feedback
Ask • Did the teacher return to the learning intention and success criteria to ensure students' understanding? • How did students engage with the learning intention and success criteria? Did they ask questions? Could they successfully paraphrase the learning intention and success criteria? What evidence shows their engagement? • What could the teacher have done to engage students who appeared uninterested in the lesson? • How did the teacher create opportunities for all students to show they were engaged? • Did the teacher check for understanding? If so, what checks did the teacher use to determine if the students understood the learning intention and success criteria? • What could the teacher do for students whose understanding is unclear?	*(Duration: 5m, 20s)* Students wrote the learning intention and success criteria in their notebooks. With a partner, they then paraphrased both the learning intention and success criteria. They wrote the paraphrasing in their notebooks. Ms. Smith called on three students to read the learning intention and success criteria to their peers. As students read their paraphrased learning intention and success criteria out loud, Ms. Smith encouraged students to jot down any words their peers offered to their paraphrasing. If there's time, I might suggest that Ms. Smith ask a student to write his or her paraphrased learning intention and success criteria under hers on the white easel in the front of the room.

Model (Questions on tiering and scaffolding omitted.)
• Did the teacher show the students what to do or tell them what to do?
• Explain how the teacher showed students how to achieve the success criteria.
• What differentiation dynamics did the teacher use to ensure he or she was doing the following?
  • Meeting individual learning styles
  • Grouping students by shared interest, topic, or ability
  • Assessing students' learning using a variety of formative assessments
  • Managing the classroom to create a safe and supportive environment
  • Continually adjusting content to meet student needs
	(Duration: 3m, 40s)
	
	Ms. Smith gave each student the short story.
	
	Students worked in groups of three.
	
	She distributed a one-page handout to students that showed what they were going to do for this lesson.
	
	• The handout showed a correctly cited piece of evidence from the story.
	
	• In the middle of the handout was a T-chart that had an example of evidence and why that evidence was important (such as: what possible inferences could be made?).

- The last third of the handout was a brief analysis paragraph connecting the evidence to the inference and why that was important.

She explained that each success criterion connected to one of the examples on the handout. Students could see what each success criterion would look like upon completion.

She encouraged students to use this handout as a model when they began their own work.

(Duration: 1un)

She emphasized that the day's lesson was a practice opportunity and they would be doing more work like correctly citing evidence and writing analysis in the future.

While Ms. Smith encouraged students to ask questions from their group members and from her, I recommend she also briefly explain that this work is a process and, like any process, encourage students not to become frustrated if the work is slow. They are learning these new skills, and it takes time.

Students appeared comfortable in groups and knew their group members.

Encourage
- How did the teacher encourage students to participate? Was the encouragement focused on fostering a growth mindset, or did it focus on offering praise?
- Did students encourage each other? If so, how? If not, why not?
- What was the teacher's final suggestion or comment to students that promotes an encouraging attitude?

Final Thoughts

The first ten minutes gave students a brief overview of the work for the day. Upon entering the class, students knew where to look for the learning intention and success criteria and began writing it in their notebooks. They felt comfortable paraphrasing the learning intention and success criteria and often jotted down new language from their peers. Ms. Smith briefly explained what the students would do that day, offering them a model so they had a reference.

Guiding Questions	Observations and Feedback
Focus • Were the learning intention and success criteria clearly visible to all students? • Were the learning intention and success criteria written in student-friendly language? • Did the teacher establish the learning target and success criteria with the students? If so, how? • How did the teacher know if the students knew and understood today's expectations? What evidence did the teacher have to support that belief?	The easel stayed in the same place during the lesson. Ms. Smith focused back to the learning intention and success criteria once at the end of the lesson. I recommend she bring students back to the learning intention and success criteria in the middle of the lesson and at the end of the lesson so students can self-assess and determine if they are meeting the success criteria.
Reach • Did the teacher offer a greeting to each student? If so, what type (verbal greeting, handshake, brief conversation)? • How did students respond to the teacher? Did they appear to feel welcome and comfortable, or did they show reluctance or anxiety? • Is there something else the teacher could do to demonstrate a classroom community?	Ms. Smith reached out to students in a variety of ways: 1. She greeted students by name as she stopped at their table. 2. She stopped at each group and listened to students reading and discussing. 3. She offered feedback as necessary. 4. She interrupted the reading twice to ask students questions to determine their understanding. However, these were basic recall questions and did not inspire critical thinking.
Ask • Did the teacher return to the learning intention and success criteria to ensure students' understanding? • How did students engage with the learning intention and success criteria? Did they ask questions? Could they successfully paraphrase the learning intention and success criteria? What evidence shows their engagement? • What could the teacher have done to engage students who appeared uninterested in the lesson?	Ms. Smith offered a brief background on Ray Bradbury and asked students about their interest in science fiction and fantasy. Many students mentioned Harry Potter and the Marvel comics as texts they have read or films they have seen. Students read the short story aloud or silently with their group. I recommend Ms. Smith bring students back to the learning intention and success criteria in the middle of the lesson and at the end of the lesson so students

• How did the teacher create opportunities for all students to show they were engaged? • Did the teacher check for understanding? If so, what checks did the teacher use to determine if the students understood the learning intention and success criteria? • What could the teacher do for students whose understanding is unclear?	can self-assess and determine if they are meeting the success criteria. As she visited groups, Ms. Smith answered any questions and encouraged students to look to their partners for assistance. She distributed a list of clarifying and probing questions to students in case they needed extra support when working in their groups.

Model (Tiering and scaffolding questions omitted.)
• Did the teacher show the students what to do or tell them what to do?
• Explain how the teacher showed students how to achieve the success criteria.
• What differentiation dynamics did the teacher use to ensure he or she was doing the following?
  • Meeting individual learning styles
  • Grouping students by shared interest, topic, or ability
  • Assessing students' learning using a variety of formative assessments
  • Managing the classroom to create a safe and supportive environment
  • Continually adjusting content to meet student needs
	Ms. Smith distributed a blank graphic organizer (T-chart) for students to write on.
	
	She modeled more specifically during this time; referring to the one-page handout and the examples on it.
	
	She read the evidence to the students out loud and explained why that evidence was important. Then she explained that the left side of the T-chart was meant for the evidence and the right side for their Why? (What possible inferences could be made?)
	
	She focused their attention on the analysis paragraph and explained they should use their Why? and inferences to create a well-written paragraph utilizing sophisticated language with critical thought.
	
	Some of the differentiation techniques she used were:
	1. Small groups
	2. Applying the model to ensure accuracy
	3. Offering clarifying and probing questions

Continued ▶

Figure 4.3: FRAME peer observation and feedback form for teachers—implementing FRAME during the lesson.

Guiding Questions	Observations and Feedback
	Ms. Smith listened to students' conversations, offering feedback and taking notes.
	During the reading, Ms. Smith interrupted students twice and asked basic recall questions to determine if students needed more support. I recommend more open-ended questions to heighten critical thinking skills.
	To differentiate, offer students two or three choices of a short story; not just one.
	Give students a chance to talk to other peers and share their T-charts with other students; not just their other two group members.
Encourage • How did the teacher encourage students to participate? Was the encouragement focused on fostering a growth mindset, or did it focus on offering praise? • Did students encourage each other? If so, how? If not, why not? • What was the teacher's final suggestion or comment to students that promotes an encouraging attitude?	When she interrupted class and asked specific questions, she commented on the "excellent evidence" students were using as a basis for their analysis. However, I encourage her to use a different word. What makes the evidence "excellent"? Instead of complimenting the evidence, praise some of the ways students used the evidence or explained the evidence. Ms. Smith assured students, again, that this was practice and they would have the opportunity to revise their work; noting the value of the process to the students.

Final Thoughts

Overall, classroom instruction was differentiated, but I recommend using more strategies to increase differentiation. Students had a model as a reference and could base their work off their model and the support of their peers. While students were engaged and enthusiastic during the lesson, recommendations were made about applying higher-order-thinking skills.

Focus

Ms. Smith explained that she always writes the learning intention and success criteria the night before and uses the white easel as the focal point for that important information. She clarified that by writing the learning intention and success criteria the night before, she feels much more organized the next morning—she knows what she wants her students to know and be able to do and is ready to start class with that learning intention in mind. She also described that she had used the white easel since the first day of school so students knew where to find that information.

I commented that I liked her approach and would be using her idea to incorporate the easel going forward. I also complimented her on her ability to refocus students toward the learning intention and success criteria but noted that her refocus occurred at the end of the lesson. I encouraged her to make a directed effort to interrupt class during the lesson so students could determine what success criteria they had mastered. I explained that I often refocused students to the learning intention and success criteria twice during my classes so students could self-assess instead of relying exclusively on me, something Ms. Smith immediately realized she hadn't done. She admitted she was so engrossed in students' reading the short story and focusing on their evidence and inference, she hadn't stopped so students could self-assess. She made a note on her copy of the "FRAME Peer Observation and Feedback Form for Teachers" to focus on this for the next lesson.

Reach

Ms. Smith knows how important it is for each student to hear his or her name as a sign of respect and reverence. She admitted that there is often a line to enter her classroom, but she believes in the value of talking with each student individually and following up every day on yesterday's brief discussion.

During class, Ms. Smith talked to each group, again using students' names, asking questions, making comments, and listening to students read. She used the catch-and-release technique to ask questions, and she jotted down notes based on students' conversations, telling several students that she would be using their notes as review questions for tomorrow.

I agreed that these were all excellent ways to reach out to her students, but I mentioned that, during class, Ms. Smith's questions were basic recall questions, like, "*Who are the main characters?*" and "*How did William treat Margot?*" I suggested that she ask questions that generate higher-level critical thinking or more open-ended questions that require a more thoughtful response. Ms. Smith agreed and said that she would like to meet again to focus on discussing open-ended questions and collaborating on a lesson using open-ended questions. We set up a date for a future meeting to do this work.

Ask

Ms. Smith always has students work on this component of FRAME in pairs or small groups. She encourages students to jot down the paraphrasing of their peers, and she ensures students know that the expertise is already in the room. If someone in her class worded the learning intention and success criteria in a more comprehensive way, she wants her students to write it down. This kind of student collaboration creates a safe space where students know they can share ideas and suggestions and other students will actively listen.

Knowing that she had successfully implemented the ask component, instead of offering direct feedback, I asked her what evidence she had that demonstrated applying the ask component. She thought about it and called attention to how she distributed clarifying and probing questions in case some students needed extra support when discussing the story with their peers. She also highlighted that as she was talking with each group and each student, she was able to check for understanding and support those students who had questions or seemed unclear about the story. She explained that as part of this process, she also took detailed notes and that these helped her focus on this specific component, since she wrote down what students were saying and could use their conversation in review for the next day's work. I agreed and said that it was clear to see that all students were engaged in the task of reading, speaking, writing, or listening.

Model

Ms. Smith successfully modeled the lesson during the first ten minutes by giving students a handout and succinctly explaining the handout and how to use it. This time was meant to introduce students to the work they would be doing, but not to go into depth until students began the lesson.

As we moved to the modeling component of FRAME during the lesson, I asked Ms. Smith to choose specific guiding questions she wanted to talk about, and since she wanted me to specifically take notes on differentiation within her classroom, did she think this lesson was differentiated for her students? She offered several ways she differentiated this lesson: small groups, clarifying and probing questions, and a completed model of the work expected.

I asked Ms. Smith if she felt she had met individual learning styles during the lesson. Again, Ms. Smith paused and read notes from the "FRAME for Peer Observation and Feedback Form for Teachers." She mentioned that students were able to work at their own pace, that she had given students the option of working in a group, and that she gave students the choice of reading the story aloud or silently.

As she looked at the components on the "FRAME for Peer Observation and Feedback Form for Teachers," Ms. Smith commented that she had not grouped students by shared interest, topic, or ability. Instead, students formed small groups of their own choosing. We also talked about the possibility of next time offering students two or three stories to choose from instead of giving every student the same one. Then, students would have the opportunity to read a story based on a shared interest or topic. In addition, I encouraged Ms. Smith to have stories of varying reading levels for students who needed extra support or who would benefit from more advanced texts. Ms. Smith said that this lesson would be a practice lesson and that she would use it again, incorporating these differentiations. I explained I had several short stories that I would be happy to share with her and she could determine if those might work the next time she wanted to teach this lesson.

Ms. Smith also commented that, as she was observing students, she was indeed informally assessing them, but not necessarily using a "variety of formative assessments." She realized she had talked with the students and had read their T-charts, but students hadn't been able to share their T-charts with anyone but their group. For the next day's review, Ms. Smith decided she wouldn't demonstrate the review, but rather ask students to partner with two other students and share their T-chart. Students, then, would have the opportunity to read what their peers wrote and prove the point of their inference. We concluded that Ms. Smith's classroom is indeed differentiated but that she could do more to hone her skill continually for the sake of her students.

Encourage

In the first ten minutes of class, Ms. Smith explained she would walk around the room and offer assistance. In addition, she explained the work students were doing in class was a practice, which for some students helped to alleviate anxiety. These were all very successful uses of the encourage component to lead off the class.

During class, she commented specifically on the "excellent" evidence she had seen on the various graphic organizers; but, she didn't ask *why* the students used that evidence. Because *excellent* is an empty word with many connotations, I encouraged

Ms. Smith to focus on the process of the work. That said, she did emphasize to students the work was practice and explained to them that they would be able to revise, demonstrating the value of the process.

When I asked how well she thought she emphasized the traits of a growth mindset with her students, she also realized she was using phrases like, "Good job" or "Nice work," when talking with individual students, but not consistently asking them *how* they achieved those labels. I agreed that while she did offer encouragement to many students, that a focus on the process about the work was most important.

Finally, I asked Ms. Smith if she thought this process was helpful to her and her teaching. She answered with an enthusiastic "Yes!" and stated how excited she was to incorporate what we had discussed. She noted that she was particularly proud of how she had created a "safe and supportive environment," how well her students worked together, and how much they supported each other's work and tried to help each other when unclear on how to proceed. We agreed to set up two more observations to support her and the valuable work she was doing with her students, and we set up an opportunity for her to observe my class in the future, as I was eager to get feedback from her to benefit my own instruction.

Conclusion

Creating opportunities to support your students is essential in providing the best educational experience possible. But, without your colleagues and peers, that experience falls short. Peer review and subsequent discussion are "valuable tools that a school or district can use to enhance teachers' pedagogical skills and develop a culture of collaboration" (Marzano, 2011, p. 81); these tools build teacher efficacy and ultimately teacher leadership. Keeping classroom doors open encourages preparation and welcomes your fellow educators to come in and observe, offering you insightful introspection and critical feedback. While opening up your classroom doors also means you're to some degree "welcoming" evaluation, you can eliminate the negative language and mindset connected with evaluation by using the "FRAME Peer Observation and Feedback Form for Teachers." This tool gives teachers a way to ignite meaningful dialogue on what they deem important to their students and a way to respectfully and humbly honor the craft of intuitive contemplation.

Do-Now Suggestions for Your Classroom or Collaborative Team

Reflect on the following suggestions and questions in collaborative teams or as individual teachers to support your work and conversations around implementing the FRAME model.

- Explain how an open-door policy, for some teachers, could cause apprehension; but also, explain why it is so important to have such a policy.

- Have you shared lessons with colleagues? If so, explain the process and what made the process a positive or negative experience. If it was negative, what could you and your colleagues do differently to make it positive?

- Preparing for peer observation is critical to the success of an observation. Discuss the value of preparing for a peer observation and the methods you might use to ensure success.

- Have you ever had a peer observe your in-class instruction? If so, explain the process. What was positive about it? What could be improved by using the "FRAME Peer Observation and Feedback Form for Teachers"?

- Share some thoughts or suggestions for your next peer observation.

FRAME Lesson and Feedback Tools

In this appendix, I offer a series of FRAME lesson and feedback tools that can enhance your work with FRAME. Over the next several pages, you will find the following.

- **FRAME peer observation and feedback form for teachers (figure A.1, pages 105–107):** Use this form to continue honing your skills using FRAME with your instruction.

- **FRAME lesson template—blank (figure A.2, pages 108–109):** This is a blank lesson template to help you structure the components of FRAME for all grade levels and reflect on its implementation.

- **FRAME lesson example—elementary school mathematics (figure A.3, pages 110–112):** This sample illustrates a single day's lesson utilizing FRAME during the first ten minutes of class.

- **FRAME lesson example—middle school English language arts day one (figure A.4, pages 113–115):** This sample illustrates the structured first ten minutes of class for day one of a two-day lesson in English language arts.

- **FRAME lesson example—middle school English language arts day two (figure A.5, pages 116–117):** This sample illustrates the structured first ten minutes of class for day two of a two-day lesson in an English language arts.

- **FRAME lesson example—high school humanities day one (figure A.6, pages 118–120):** This sample illustrates the structured first ten minutes of class for day one of a two-day lesson in humanities.

- **FRAME lesson example—high school humanities day two (figure A.7, pages 121–123):** This sample illustrates the structured first ten minutes of class for day two of a two-day lesson in humanities.

Guiding Questions	Observations and Feedback
Focus • Were the learning intention and success criteria clearly visible to all students? • Were the learning intention and success criteria written in student-friendly language? • Did the teacher establish the learning intention and success criteria with the students? If so, how? • How did the teacher know if the students knew and understood today's expectations? What evidence did the teacher have to support that belief?	
Reach • Did the teacher offer a greeting to each student? If so, what type (verbal greeting, handshake, brief conversation)? • How did students respond to the teacher? Did they appear to feel welcome and comfortable, or did they show reluctance or anxiety? • Is there something else the teacher could do to demonstrate a classroom community?	

Continued ▶

Figure A.1: FRAME peer observation and feedback form for teachers.

Guiding Questions	Observations and Feedback
Ask • Did the teacher return to the learning intention and success criteria to ensure students' understanding? • How did students engage with the learning intention and success criteria? Did they ask questions? Could they successfully paraphrase the learning intention and success criteria? What evidence shows their engagement? • What could the teacher have done to engage students who appeared uninterested in the lesson? • How did the teacher create opportunities for all students to show they were engaged? • Did the teacher check for understanding? If so, what checks did the teacher use to determine if the students understood the learning intention and success criteria? • What could the teacher do for students whose understanding is unclear?	

Model
 	
• Did the teacher show the students what to do or tell them what to do?
 	
• Explain how the teacher showed students how to achieve the success criteria.
 	
• What differentiation dynamics did the teacher use to ensure he or she was doing the following?
  • Meeting individual learning styles
  • Grouping students by shared interest, topic, or ability
  • Assessing students' learning using a variety of formative assessments
  • Managing the classroom to create a safe and supportive environment
  • Continually adjusting content to meet student needs	

- What tiering techniques did the teacher use to ensure he or she was doing the following?
  - Developing varying levels of complexity of the task
  - Offering various degrees of direction for students needing additional support
  - Creating opportunities for equity among student work
- What scaffolding systems did the teacher use to ensure he or she was doing the following?
  - Building on the prior knowledge a learner has of a particular topic
  - Creating opportunities for peer collaboration and learning
  - Designing an environment where students are free to ask questions and challenge thinking in a respectful, culturally sensitive way

Encourage

- How did the teacher encourage students to participate? Was the encouragement focused on fostering a growth mindset, or did it focus on offering praise?
- Did students encourage each other? If so, how? If not, why not?
- What was the teacher's final suggestion or comment to students that promotes an encouraging attitude?

Final Thoughts

Visit go.SolutionTree.com/instruction for a free reproducible version of this figure.

Lesson title or topic:	
Number of days for the lesson:	
Focus (before your students walk in the door): Create a learning intention and success criteria in student-friendly language.	**Learning intention:** **Success criteria:** I know I am successful because—
Debrief and comments (fill out after lesson):	
Reach (before your students walk in the door): List some ways to acknowledge students as they each walk in the room.	
Debrief and comments (fill out after lesson):	
Ask (three to four minutes): List some clarifying and probing questions you will ask students. (Clarifying and probing questions help students analyze the "So what?" of the learning intention and success criteria.)	

Debrief and comments (fill out after lesson):		
Model (five to six minutes): Give an overview of the assignment. If applicable, give students a visual example of the process and final product.		
Debrief and comments (fill out after lesson):		
Encourage (one minute): Encourage the work by praising the process. List some key points that remind students of the importance of productive struggle.		
Debrief and comments (fill out after lesson):		

Figure A.2: FRAME lesson template—blank.

Visit go.SolutionTree.com/instruction for a free reproducible version of this figure.

Lesson title or topic: Adding and subtracting numbers up to 100

Number of days for the lesson: One day (approximately seventy minutes)

Focus (before your students walk in the door): Create a learning intention and success criteria in student-friendly language.	**Learning intention:** *I can show my understanding of adding and subtracting numbers within 100.* **Success criteria:** I know I am successful because— • *I can show my understanding of adding and subtracting numbers within 100 using drawings and equations.* • *I can write addition and subtraction equations with missing addends.* • *I can explain that the equal sign means "the same number as" when I write equations.*

Debrief and comments (fill out after lesson):
I wrote the learning intention and the success criteria during my prep period the day before. I wrote it on a Google slide for easy access for each lesson.

Reach (before your students walk in the door): List some ways to acknowledge students as they each walk in the room.	• *Meet the students at our line, and say hello to each of them.* • *Turn on the music, and display a fun, positive Bitmoji and a GIF on a Google slide.*

Debrief and comments (fill out after lesson):
Today, I chose to wear my silly hat and sunglasses as I stood outside the door, and my students loved it. I received several hugs and high fives! I want kids begging to come to school to see what happens next and be fully engaged with the learning. A silly hat with sunglasses helps build a culture where students feel comfortable and want to learn.
Also, today I played "Believer" by Imagine Dragons as students walked into class. This connects to our classroom culture since we are the Believers (the teacher-created classroom inspirational name) building a classroom community.

Ask (three to four minutes): List some clarifying and probing questions you will ask students. (Clarifying and probing questions help students analyze the "So what?" of the learning intention and success criteria.)

- *Give students time to ask questions to ensure understanding.*
- *Ask students to try to anticipate the problems they may have when doing the work.*
- *Provide a sentence starter for students who might want one: I had a productive struggle because _____, so I _____.*

Debrief and comments (fill out after lesson):

Here were some of their questions.
- *"Can we use base 10 blocks?"*
- *"Can we use expanded form?"*
- *"Can we use the opposite of subtraction to solve the problem?"*

One of the students used the sentence starter and said, "I had a productive struggle because I was having trouble subtracting correctly, so I used base 10 blocks to solve the subtraction problem."

Model (five to six minutes): Give an overview of the assignment. If applicable, give students a visual example of the process and final product.

- *Model the fishbowl method to show how they are to share their strategies to solve the subtraction or addition problem.*
  - *Choose four students to share their addition and subtraction strategies and purposeful sentence stems. The rest of the class sits around the four modeling students to observe and understand the expectations.*
  - *Then put students into groups of four and have them use the fishbowl method.*

Figure A.3: FRAME lesson example—elementary school mathematics.

Continued ▶

Debrief and comments (fill out after lesson):

They used sentence stems to clarify, agree, and disagree. I also modeled how to use positive affirmations when their partners shared their strategies.

Here are some things they shared during the fishbowl.

- "I had a productive struggle with understanding whether to add or subtract."
- "I persevered when I tried two different ways to solve the problem."

During this time, I always stress the importance of a growth mindset and encourage my students to try something new. My students understand a growth mindset means to be willing to try something new. They understand they must persevere when they are having a productive struggle. They are used to this type of learning. They also understand that just because they might have struggled with mathematics previously, it does not mean they will always struggle.

Encourage (one minute): Encourage the work by praising the process. List some key points that remind students of the importance of productive struggle.

- Have them reflect on their learning using a 1–4 continuum.

Debrief and comments (fill out after lesson):

In my class, we discuss the importance of thinking about our learning. Students rate themselves on a daily basis using a 1–4 continuum. They have to explain why they are having a productive struggle and what they can do to get more help. I seldom answer their questions directly but rather ask them more questions; since math is inquiry, I always tell my students you don't have to get the correct answer right away. But I encourage them to stick with the problem and use the various strategies.

Source: © 2019 by Tika Epstein, elementary teacher, Keith and Karen Hayes Elementary School, Las Vegas, Nevada. Adapted with permission.

Lesson title or topic: Using commas correctly in writing

Number of days for the lesson: Five days (thirty-five minutes per class period)

Focus (before your students walk in the door): Create a learning intention and success criteria in student-friendly language.	Learning intention:
	I can use commas correctly using the book Eats, Shoots and Leaves: Why, Commas Really Do Make a Difference! (Truss, 2006).
	Success criteria:
	I know I am successful because—
	• I can (determine) figure out how comma usage changes the meaning of sentences.
	• I can (apply) use the Comma Rules Master sheet in my own writing.
	• I can practice using commas in different sentence examples.
	• I can (analyze) review my writing and know when to use commas in any writing.

Debrief and comments (fill out after lesson):

I wrote the learning intention and the success criteria before I left for home the day before. The learning intention and success criteria will stay the same for as long as the lesson will take. I posted it on the back wall and referred to it several times throughout the lesson so students could check their understanding and determine whether they achieved the success criteria yet and, if not, what they needed from me to get there.

But for these particular success criteria, I also wanted to stretch their academic vocabulary, so I included more scholarly language in parentheses.

I also wrote the probing questions on the board in case they needed these when paraphrasing the learning intention and success criteria. I thought it might help students brainstorm.

Figure A.4: FRAME lesson example—middle school English language arts day one.

Continued ▶

Reach (before your students walk in the door): List some ways to acknowledge students as they each walk in the room.	• Meet students in the hallway and offer a greeting. • If students don't return the greeting, do it again.

Debrief and comments (fill out after lesson):

I met students in the hallway and greeted them as they came into the room. I noticed in the past that some students walk right past me without returning a greeting (maybe middle school students think they're too cool to say hi to their teacher?), so, in these cases, I repeated my greeting to them and prompted them to return my greeting. It's important that students realize that the greeting is a social skill, and encouraging them to say something back helps strengthen that skill.

Ask (three to four minutes): List some clarifying and probing questions you will ask students. (Clarifying and probing questions help students analyze the "So what?" of the learning intention and success criteria.)	• Introduce the learning intention and success criteria. • Ask students to paraphrase the learning intention and success criteria (show students the probing questions on the board; they can use these to help them paraphrase). • Ask students to write down their paraphrased learning intention and success criteria in their notebooks.

Debrief and comments (fill out after lesson):

I referred back to the learning intention and success criteria throughout the class period, since it provided a good point of reference. It especially helped students with attention issues because they could see how they're making progress.

Some of the student paraphrases were:

I can figure out how comma usage changes the meaning of sentences.
• "When I look at a sentence, I can figure out how it changes when the comma gets moved."

I can use the Comma Rules Master sheet in my own writing.
• "Putting the commas in the right places when I write."

I can practice using commas in different sentence examples.
• "I can read different sentences and put the commas in where they go, not just once but over and over again."

I can review my writing and know when to use commas in my writing.
• "I can check my work to see if I am missing the commas."

• "Analyze is like a detective who checks for clues to figure out if he's right, right?"

Model (five to six minutes): Give an overview of the assignment. If applicable, give students a visual example of the process and final product.	• Hold up the book *Eats, Shoots and Leaves* (Truss, 2006) so students can see this will be their resource. • Show them examples of different types of sentences. • Explain that we will learn how to use commas correctly in these examples.
Debrief and comments: *I didn't use much time here, since I just wanted to show them a variety of sentences without commas and give an overall explanation of what we would be working on.*	
Encourage (one minute): Encourage the work by praising the process. List some key points that remind students of the importance of productive struggle.	• Explain that for many students, understanding comma rules and using commas can take time, so if we need more time, that will be OK. • Explain that we will keep practicing until they feel comfortable with the grammar rules.
Debrief and comments: *For some students, grammar can seem really difficult because they might not have had much practice. I wanted them to know that this is not a rush and that we would keep practicing this skill so they feel comfortable using commas.*	

Source: © 2019 by Jackie Bladow, middle school teacher, Dyer Intermediate School, Burlington, Wisconsin. Adapted with permission.

Lesson title or topic: Using commas correctly in writing

Number of days for the lesson: Five days (thirty-five minutes per class period)

Focus (before your students walk in the door): Create a learning intention and success criteria in student-friendly language.	**Learning intention:** I can use commas correctly using the book *Eats, Shoots and Leaves: Why, Commas Really Do Make a Difference!* (Truss, 2006). **Success criteria:** I know I am successful because— • I can (determine) figure out how comma usage changes the meaning of sentences. • I can (apply) use the Comma Rules Master sheet in my own writing. • I can practice using commas in different sentence examples. • I can (analyze) review my writing and know when to use commas in any writing.

Debrief and comments (fill out after lesson): *I used the same learning intention and success criteria for the five-day lesson and kept the probing questions on the board until the end of today's lesson.*

Reach (before your students walk in the door): List some ways to acknowledge students as they each walk in the room.	• Meet students in the hallway and offer a greeting. • If students don't return the greeting, do it again.

Debrief and comments (fill out after lesson): *I continued to reach out to all of my students. I often asked questions about what they did the night before or if they had any weekend plans—anything to spark personal conversation.*

Ask (three to four minutes): List some clarifying and probing questions you will ask students. (Clarifying and probing questions help students analyze the "So what?" of the learning intention and success criteria.)	• Ask four students to read the paraphrased learning intention and success criteria they created the day before.

Debrief and comments: *I continued to refer back to the learning intention and success criteria throughout the class period, since it provided a good point of reference.*

Model (five to six minutes): Give an overview of the assignment. If applicable, give students a visual example of the process and final product.

- *Ask three students to write an example of a sentence using the correct comma rule from their own writing.*

Debrief and comments (fill out after lesson):

I wanted students to show examples of the work they had done yesterday so they could see a part of the process. Knowing that we would be working on this today, I wanted them to realize that this was just a part of what we would be learning, and there was more to come.

Encourage (one minute): Encourage the work by praising the process. List some key points that remind students of the importance of productive struggle.

- *Encourage students to share their thinking and problem-solving skills with their peers.*

Debrief and comments (fill out after lesson):

I tried to make sure each student has the opportunity to help or support another student. By doing that, all students recognize that their peers have something to share.

Source: © 2019 by Jackie Bladow, middle school teacher, Dyer Intermediate School, Burlington, Wisconsin. Adapted with permission.

Figure A.5: FRAME lesson example—middle school English language arts day two.

Lesson title or topic: Learning to prewrite an Origins, Purpose, Content, Value, Limits (OPCVL) essay

Number of days for the lesson: Two days (ninety-minute blocks)

Focus (before your students walk in the door): Create a learning intention and success criteria in student-friendly language.	**Learning intention:** *I can learn to prewrite for an Origins, Purpose, Context, Value, Limits (OPCVL) essay, utilizing Dr. Seuss's political cartoons as a source.* **Success criteria:** *I know I am successful because—* • *I can identify subtle inferences utilizing Dr. Seuss's cartoons and explain how those inferences might have influenced readers.* • *I can analyze Dr. Seuss's cartoons and critique the bias and stereotyping associated with his cartoons.* • *I can prewrite an OPCVL using Dr. Seuss's political cartoons as a source.*

Debrief and comments (fill out after lesson):
I wrote the learning intention and the success criteria during my prep period the day before. I wrote it on the sideboard; that area is designated for the learning intention and success criteria.

Reach (before your students walk in the door): List some ways to acknowledge students as they each walk in the room.	• *Stand outside the door and ask questions and follow-up questions of each student (as many as I can) to create a connection (for example, "Did you win the soccer game last night?" or "How was your evening?").*

Debrief and comments (fill out after lesson):
I think students appreciate it when I get to know them in a more personal way because as the year goes on, they're excited to share news with me. That personal connection is so important, especially in high school, because I want students to know they can come to me if they need someone to talk to.

Ask (three to four minutes): List some clarifying and probing questions you will ask students. (Clarifying and probing questions help students analyze the "So what?" of the learning intention and success criteria.)

- Introduce the learning intention and the first two bullets of the success criteria only, focusing on these key words: identify, inferences, explain, analyze.
- Introduce the final bullet tomorrow.
- Assign each team a success criteria bullet point (except for the final bullet), and ask them to write it down in their notebook.
- Within their teams, ask students to discuss that bullet point in their own words and write it in their notebooks.
- Ask students to share out their responses.

Debrief and comments (fill out after lesson):

Unpacking the success criteria really helped my students understand that they weren't just going to be sharing their opinions about political cartoons but really looking closely at what the cartoon was saying and what it wasn't saying. In addition, political cartoons are loaded with bias, so I wanted them to notice that bias and be able to discuss why it's there.

I asked students to define what the key words in the success criteria meant to make sure we were all on the same page. Here are my questions and some of their answers.

- What's an inference, and how can I identify inferences?
  - "When I think of an inference, I think of a guess."
  - "But it has to be an informed guess. I just can't make it up."
  - "I can identify them by looking at what the cartoon is saying and then guessing what he (the artist) actually means."
- Why is it important to explain the inferences?
  - "So other people know what you're talking about."
  - "My inference might be different from somebody else's, so I want that person to explain why."
- What does analyze mean, and why should we analyze?
  - "Analyze is a deeper meaning of something."
  - "It's like how I look at a painting in art. I have to take it apart in art and talk about it."
  - "Tells the main idea."

Figure A.6: FRAME lesson example—high school humanities day one.

Continued ▶

Model (five to six minutes): Give an overview of the assignment. If applicable, give students a visual example of the process and final product.

- Show students a political cartoon by Dr. Seuss without his name on it and ask students what they notice about the stylization of the cartoon.
- Briefly explain to students that we will be analyzing several of Dr. Seuss's cartoons and discussing their political implications during World War II.

Debrief and comments (fill out after lesson):

A couple of students noticed that it "kinda looked like the characters from Dr. Seuss's books." Overall, students were surprised that Dr. Seuss created political cartoons and were interested in seeing more cartoons about his views.

Encourage (one minute): Encourage the work by praising the process. List some key points that remind students of the importance of productive struggle.

- Be positive, but make sure to keep students focused on the cartoon and not get sidetracked by Dr. Seuss books.

Debrief and comments (fill out after lesson):

I noticed, during the model component, a couple of students were trying hard to analyze the cartoon and, as a result, their thoughts were a little off-base and seemed to confuse their peers. I told them, "I hear what you're saying, but let's try not to overthink it, either." I appreciate it when students take risks and are willing to share their thoughts with the class, but I don't want them to overreach, either. When offering encouragement in this particular lesson, I wanted students to notice details, such as symbols and author bias, so I encouraged them to keep digging and detect things they hadn't focused on before.

Source: © 2019 by Joe Koester, high school humanities teacher, Ronald Reagan IB High School, Milwaukee, Wisconsin. Adapted with permission.

Lesson title or topic: Learning to prewrite an Origins, Purpose, Content, Value, Limits (OPCVL) essay

Number of days for the lesson: Two days (ninety-minute blocks)

Focus (before your students walk in the door): Create a learning intention and success criteria in student-friendly language.	**Learning intention:** I can learn to prewrite for an Origins, Purpose, Context, Value, Limits (OPCVL) essay, utilizing Dr. Seuss's political cartoons as a source. **Success criteria:** I know I am successful because— • I can identify subtle inferences utilizing Dr. Seuss's cartoons and explain how those inferences might have influenced readers. • I can analyze Dr. Seuss's cartoons and critique the bias and stereotyping associated with his cartoons. • <u>I can prewrite an OPCVL using Dr. Seuss's political cartoons as a source.</u>

Debrief and comments (fill out after lesson):
While I used the same learning intention and success criteria since they covered the entire lesson, I did underline and box the last criterion since we were going to spend this specific class period prewriting our OPCVL using a Dr. Seuss political cartoon.

Reach (before your students walk in the door): List some ways to acknowledge students as they each walk in the room.	• *Stand outside the door and ask questions and follow-up questions of each student (as many as I can) to create a connection.*

Debrief and comments:
I continue to reach out to all of my students in as many personal ways as possible.

Figure A.7: FRAME lesson example—high school humanities day two.

Continued ▶

Ask (three to four minutes): List some clarifying and probing questions you will ask students. (Clarifying and probing questions help students analyze the "So what?" of the learning intention and success criteria.)

- Ask three students to read their paraphrased learning intention and success criteria they had created the day before for review of our work.
- Ask all teams to explain the connection between an OPCVL and their comments.

Debrief and comments (fill out after lesson):

I'm glad I spent the extra minute to have students read their paraphrased learning intention and success criteria from yesterday. It gave students another opportunity to remind them of what we were going to do.

I asked students: What is the connection between an OPCVL and identify, explain, and analyze? Take a look at the comments you wrote down from yesterday.

- "Yesterday, when we were looking at the cartoon, we identified who drew it and when it was drawn. We were also able to figure out the purpose of the cartoon."
- "When I looked at the cartoon and analyzed it, I was able to figure out whom it had value to, like the Americans, their allies, or certain other people. You know, that kind of stuff."
- "Yesterday, my group figured out some limitations of the cartoon, like, Was Dr. Seuss biased? Then we thought we'd probably write the OPCVL and connect what we talked about yesterday to our paper."

Model (five to six minutes): Give an overview of the assignment. If applicable, give students a visual example of the process and final product.

- Show the PowerPoint slide with the graphic organizer.
- Explain they will use this graphic organizer to brainstorm their OPCVL. This will be their prewriting document.
- Ask students to collaborate with their teams and answer each question in relation to the cartoon they are about to receive from use.
- Show students a completed brainstorming chart.
- Distribute a new Dr. Seuss political cartoon to each table along with a list of active verbs for them to use in their writing.

Debrief and comments (fill out after lesson):

I wanted this modeling to be brief because I wanted their brainstorming to be as organic as possible. In addition, I knew I would be modeling throughout the lesson by offering suggestions and ideas. But, initially, I didn't want to overload them during the first ten minutes. I thought too many suggestions or ideas might pigeonhole them into thinking this is what they should do or have to write. I wanted their OPCVL brainstorming to be spontaneous and natural.

Encourage (one minute): Encourage the work by praising the process. List some key points that remind students of the importance of productive struggle.

- *Remind students to stay focused on the cartoon and answer the questions using what they already know, along with some educated inferences.*

Debrief and comments (fill out after lesson):

I encouraged them to stay focused on the information that connected to the OPCVL and to use the language of a historian.

Source: © 2019 by Joe Koester, high school humanities teacher, Ronald Reagan IB High School, Milwaukee, Wisconsin. Adapted with permission.

References and Resources

Ainsworth, L., & Viegut, D. (2015). *Common formative assessments 2.0: How teacher teams intentionally align standards, instruction, and assessment.* Thousand Oaks, CA: Corwin Press.

Alber, R. (2014, January 24). 6 scaffolding strategies to use with your students. *Edutopia.* Accessed at www.edutopia.org/blog/scaffolding-lessons-six-strategies -rebecca-alber on March 26, 2019.

Allen, J. (2008). *More tools for teaching content literacy.* Portland, ME: Stenhouse.

Altman, I. (2018, January 3). Is multitasking an asset or a liability? *Forbes.* Accessed at www.forbes.com/sites/ianaltman/2018/01/03/is-multitasking-an-asset-or-a -liability/#439957a94d2f on March 26, 2019.

Anderson, L. W., & Krathwohl, D. (Eds.). (2001). *A taxonomy for learning, teaching, and assessing: A revision of Bloom's taxonomy of educational objectives.* Boston: Allyn & Bacon.

Andone, D. (2018, March 23). *What you should know about the March for Our Lives.* Accessed at www.cnn.com/2018/03/21/us/march-for-our-lives-explainer/index. html on May 21, 2019.

Archer, A. L., & Hughes, C. A. (2011). *Explicit instruction: Effective and efficient teaching.* New York: Guilford Press.

Associated Press. (2019, August 21). *Small particles of plastic have found a home in Arctic snow, scientists say.* Accessed at https://newsela.com/read/plastics-artic-snow on August 21, 2019.

Atta, M. A., & Ayaz, M. (2014). Use of teachers' eye contact in the classroom and its effect on the speculative execution of students at primary school level: A gender-based study. *Gomal University Journal of Research, 30*(1), 91–97.

Aymett, R., & Krahenbuhl, K. S. (2016, September 8). Teaching goal setting to help students take ownership of learning. *ASCD Express*, *12*(1).

Barati, L. (2015). The impact of eye-contact between teacher and student on L2 learning. *Journal of Applied Linguistics and Language Research*, *2*(7), 222–227. Accessed at www.jallr.com/index.php/JALLR/article/view/180/pdf180 on March 26, 2019.

Black, P., & Wiliam, D. (2009). Developing the theory of formative assessment. *Educational Assessment, Evaluation and Accountability*, *21*(1), 5–31.

Bloom, B. S. (Ed.). (1956). *Taxonomy of educational objectives: The classification of educational goals; Handbook I: Cognitive domain*. New York: David McKay.

Bracher, T. (2014, December 1). Top tips for surviving a teaching observation. *The Guardian*. Accessed at www.theguardian.com/education/2014/dec/01/top-tips-for -surviving-a-teaching-observation on March 26, 2019.

Bradbury, R. (1998). All summer in a day. In *A medicine for melancholy and other stories* (pp. 88–93). New York: Harper Collins.

Bramschreiber, T. (2012). Taking peer feedback to heart. *Educational Leadership*, *70*(3). Accessed at www.ascd.org/publications/educational-leadership/nov12 /vol70/num03/Taking-Peer-Feedback-to-Heart.aspx on July 28, 2019.

Bray, B., & McClaskey, K. (n.d.). *Personalization vs differentiation vs individualization*. Accessed at https://education.alberta.ca/media/3069745 /personalizationvsdifferentiationvsindividualization.pdf on October 14, 2019.

Briggs, S. (2014, October 4). *How to make learning relevant to your students (and why it's crucial to their success)*. Accessed at www.opencolleges.edu.au/informed/features /how-to-make-learning-relevant on March 26, 2019.

Britton, K. (2007, October 23). *Process praise and growth mindsets*. Accessed at https:// theanocoaching.wordpress.com/2007/10/23/process-praise-and-growth-mindsets on March 26, 2019.

Brock, A., & Hundley, H. (2018). *In other words: Phrases for growth mindset: A teachers guide to empowering students through effective praise and feedback*. Berkeley, CA: Ulysses Press.

Brontë, C. (1997). *Jane Eyre*. New York: Modern Library.

Buffum, A., Mattos, M., & Malone, J. (2018). *Taking action: A handbook for RTI at Work*. Bloomington, IN: Solution Tree Press.

Catapano, J. (n.d.). *Teaching strategies that give models, examples*. Accessed at www .teachhub.com/teaching-strategies-give-models-examples on March 26, 2019.

Chu, M. (2012). Observe, reflect, and apply: Ways to successfully mentor early childhood educators. *Dimensions of Early Childhood*, *40*(3), 20–29.

Clayton, M. K. (2010, August 18). *Displaying student work*. Accessed at www .responsiveclassroom.org/displaying-student-work on March 26, 2019.

Cook, C. R. (n.d.). *Positive greetings at the door: Proactive classroom management procedure.* Accessed at www.sjcoe.org/selparesources/tiers/Positive_Greetings_at_the_Door_script.doc.pdf on March 28, 2019.

Cook, C. R., Fiat, A., Larson, M., Daikos, C., Slemrod, T., Holland, E. A., et al. (2018). Positive greetings at the door: Evaluation of a low-cost, high-yield proactive classroom management strategy. *Journal of Positive Behavior Interventions, 20*(3), 149–159.

Cooper, K. M., Haney, B., Krieg, A., & Brownell, S. E. (2017). What's in a name? The importance of students perceiving that an instructor knows their names in a high-enrollment biology classroom. *CBE Life Sciences Education, 16*(1).

Cox, J. (n.d.a). *Differentiated instruction strategies: Tiered assignments.* Accessed at www.teachhub.com/differentiated-instruction-strategies-using-tiered-assignments on March 28, 2019.

Cox, J. (n.d.b). *Discover teaching strategies to individualize instruction.* Accessed at www.teachhub.com/discover-teaching-strategies-individualize-instruction on March 28, 2019.

Damon, A., & Laine, B. (2019, August 20). *Microplastics discovered in 'extreme' concentrations in North Atlantic.* Accessed at www.cnn.com/2019/08/19/world/microplastics-sargasso-sea-north-atlantic-intl/index.html on August 21, 2019.

Darling-Hammond, L., & Austin, K. (n.d.). *Lessons for life: Learning and transfer.* Accessed at www.learner.org/courses/learningclassroom/support/11_learning_transfer.pdf on July 31, 2019.

Davis, S. (2014, May 13). *Using Bloom's taxonomy to write learning outcomes.* Accessed at www.pearsoned.com/using-blooms-taxonomy-to-write-learning-outcomes on July 29, 2019.

Dean, C. B., Hubbell, E. R., Pitler, H., & Stone, B. (2012). *Classroom instruction that works: Research-based strategies for increasing student achievement* (2nd ed.). Alexandria, VA: Association for Supervision and Curriculum Development.

Denton, P. (2007). *Open-ended questions.* Accessed at www.responsiveclassroom.org/open-ended-questions on July 31, 2019.

Department of Education and Training. (2017). *High impact teaching strategies: Excellence in teaching and learning.* Accessed at https://www.education.vic.gov.au/Documents/school/teachers/support/highimpactteachstrat.docx on July 31, 2019.

Dweck, C. (n.d.). *What is mindset.* Accessed at https://mindsetonline.com/whatisit/about on May 21, 2019.

Dweck, C. S. (2006). *Mindset: The new psychology of success.* New York: Random House.

Eberly Center. (n.d.). *Students compartmentalize knowledge and skills and hence can't draw on them.* Accessed at www.cmu.edu/teaching/solveproblem/strat-cantapply/cantapply-06.html on March 26, 2019.

Educational Research Newsletter & Webinars. (2015, April 29). *Teacher modeling important for student engagement.* Accessed at www.ernweb.com/educational -research-articles/teacher-modeling-important-for-student-engagement on March 28, 2019.

Education World. (2017). *Minimize lecture, maximize learning: The workshop model.* Accessed at www.educationworld.com/a_curr/minimize-lecture-workshop-model .shtml on March 28, 2019.

Ehmke, R. (n.d.). *Anxiety in the classroom: What it looks like, and why it's often mistaken for something else.* Accessed at https://childmind.org/article/classroom-anxiety-in -children on March 28, 2019.

Eisenbach, B. B. (2016, February). *Student reflection: A tool for growth and development.* Accessed at www.amle.org/BrowsebyTopic/WhatsNew/WNDet/TabId/270 /ArtMID/888/ArticleID/586/Student-Reflection-A-Tool-for-Growth-and -Development.aspx on March 28, 2019.

EL Education (n.d.a) *Helping all learners: Tiering.* Accessed at https://eleducation.org /resources/helping-all-learners-tiering on August 1, 2019.

EL Education. (n.d.b). *Students discuss the power of learning targets.* Accessed at https:// eleducation.org/resources/students-discuss-the-power-of-learning-targets on March 29, 2019.

Everette, M. (2017, October 18). *The hidden power of learning objectives* [Blog post]. Accessed at www.scholastic.com/teachers/blog-posts/meghan-everette/17-18/The -Hidden-Power-of-Learning-Objectives on March 28, 2019.

Ferlazzo, L. (2017, January 14). *Response: Student goal-setting in the classroom* [Blog post]. Accessed at https://blogs.edweek.org/teachers/classroom_qa_with_larry_ ferlazzo/2017/01/student-goal-setting-in-the-classroom.html on March 28, 2019.

Fessenden, M. (2018, May 10). *U.S. capitol's Statuary Hall to get first state-commissioned statue of a black American.* Accessed at www.tweentribune.com/article/tween56 /us-capitols-statuary-hall-get-first-state-commissioned-statue-black-american on August 14, 2019.

Finley, T. (2015). *22 powerful closure activities: Quick activities that can be used to check for understanding or emphasize key information at the end of a lesson.* Accessed at www.edutopia.org/blog/22-powerful-closure-activities-todd-finley on September 10, 2019.

Firefly Education. (2017, October 18). *Get the most out of learning intentions.* Accessed at www.fireflyeducation.com.au/pd/article/get-the-most-out-of-learning-intentions on March 28, 2019.

Fisher, D., & Frey, N. (2010). Questioning to check for understanding. In *Guided instruction: How to develop confident and successful learners.* Accessed at www .ascd.org/publications/books/111017/chapters/Questioning-to-Check-for -Understanding.aspx on March 28, 2019.

Fisher, D., & Frey, N. (2018). Show & tell: A video column / A map for meaningful learning. *Educational Leadership*, *75*(5), 82–83.

Fisher, D., Frey, N., Amador, O., & Assof, J. (2019). *The teacher clarity playbook: A hands-on guide to creating learning intentions and success criteria for organized, effective instruction.* Thousand Oaks, CA: Corwin.

Flom, J. (2014, October 6). *Peer-to-peer observation: Five questions for making it work* [Blog post]. Accessed at http://inservice.ascd.org/peer-to-peer-observation-five-questions-for-making-it-work on March 28, 2019.

Freibrun, M. (2019, March 5). *Spark motivation in your students with success criteria.* Accessed at www.teachingchannel.org/tch/blog/spark-motivation-your-students-success-criteria on July 29, 2019.

Furr, A. (2016, September 21). *Mispronouncing student's name now considered a 'microaggresson.'* Accessed at www.cnsnews.com/blog/amy-furr/mispronouncing-students-name-now-considered-microaggression on August 1, 2019.

Glossary of Education Reform. (2013, August 29). *Growth mindset.* Accessed at www.edglossary.org/growth-mindset on March 28, 2019.

Gonzalez, J. (2013, October 13). *Open your door: Why we need to see each other teach* [Blog post]. Accessed at www.cultofpedagogy.com/open-your-door on March 28, 2019.

Gonzalez, J. (2014, April 14). *How we pronounce student names, and why it matters* [Blog post]. Accessed at www.cultofpedagogy.com/gift-of-pronunciation on March 28, 2019.

Gonzalez, J. (2016, March 27). *A few strategies to help slow-working students* [Blog post]. Accessed at www.cultofpedagogy.com/slow-working-students on March 28, 2019.

Gordon, S., Butters, J., Maxey, S., Ciccarelli, J., & Checkley, K. (2002). *Improving instruction through observation and feedback: Facilitator's guide.* Alexandria, VA: Association for Supervision and Curriculum Development.

Goss, P., & Sonnemann, J. (2017). *Engaging students: Creating classrooms that improve learning.* Accessed at https://pdfs.semanticscholar.org/5b89/f0296f949e270903676027fd6d9a0ef769e5.pdf on August 23, 2019.

Green, K. (2006). No novice teacher left behind: Guiding novice teachers to improve decision-making through structured questioning. *Penn GSE Perspectives on Urban Education*, *4*(1), 1–8.

Grimm, E. D., Kaufman, T., & Doty, D. (2014). Rethinking classroom observation. *Educational Leadership*, *71*(8). Accessed at www.ascd.org/publications/educational-leadership/may14/vol71/num08/Rethinking-Classroom-Observation.aspx on March 28, 2019.

Gross-Loh, C. (2016, December 16). How praise became a consolation prize. *The Atlantic.* Accessed at www.theatlantic.com/education/archive/2016/12/how-praise-became-a-consolation-prize/510845 on March 28, 2019.

Hagler, K. (2017). *Take 5! for language arts: Writing that builds critical-thinking skills (K–2)*. North Mankato, MN: Capstone.

Hamblin, J. (2015, June 30). 100 percent is overrated. *The Atlantic*. Accessed at www .theatlantic.com/education/archive/2015/06/the-s-word/397205 on March 28, 2019.

Harbour, K. E., Evanovich, L. L., Sweigart, C. A., & Hughes, L. E. (2015). A brief review of effective teaching practices that maximize student engagement. *Preventing School Failure: Alternative Education for Children and Youth, 59*(1), 5–13.

Harper, A. (2018, September 14). *New study suggests that greeting students with a positive message yields benefits*. Accessed at www.educationdive.com/news/new -study-suggests-that-greeting-students-with-a-positive-message-yields-be/532359 on March 28, 2019.

Haston, W. (2007, March 1). Teacher modeling as an effective teaching strategy. *Music Educators Journal, 93*(4), 26–30.

Hattie, J. (2012). *Visible learning for teachers: Maximizing impact on learning*. New York: Routledge.

Hawley, W., Irvine, J. J., & Landa, M. (n.d.) *Culture in the classroom*. Accessed at www.tolerance.org/professional-development/culture-in-the-classroom on July 30, 2019.

Hendry, G. D., & Oliver, G. R. (2012). Seeing is believing: The benefits of peer observation. *Journal of University Teaching & Learning Practice, 9*(1). Accessed at https://ro.uow.edu.au/jutlp/vol9/iss1/7 on March 28, 2019.

Inclusive Schools Network. (2015, August 20). *The principal's responsibilities in supporting quality instruction* [Blog post]. Accessed at https://inclusiveschools.org /the-principals-responsibilities-in-supporting-quality-instruction on March 28, 2019.

Indiana University. (2013). *Handout: Clarifying and probing questions*. Accessed at https://global.indiana.edu/documents/global-perspectives/clarifying-and-probing -questions-handout-step-2-define.pdf on March 28, 2019.

Intel Corporation. (2012). *Instructional strategies: Modeling*. Accessed at www.intel. com/content/dam/www/program/education/us/en/documents/project-design /strategies/instructionalstrategies-modeling.pdf on March 28, 2019.

IRIS Center. (n.d.) *What is instructional scaffolding?* Accessed at https://iris .peabody.vanderbilt.edu/module/sca/cresource/q1/p01 on August 1, 2019.

Jackson, R. R. (2018). *Never work harder than your students: And other principles of great teaching* (2nd ed.). Alexandria, VA: Association for Supervision and Curriculum Development.

Jason, Z. (2017, Winter). Bored out of their minds. *Harvard Ed. Magazine*. Accessed at www.gse.harvard.edu/news/ed/17/01/bored-out-their-minds on March 28, 2019.

Jensen, E. (2019). *Poor students, rich teaching: Seven high-impact mindsets for students from poverty* (Rev. ed.). Bloomington, IN: Solution Tree Press.

Kelly, M. (2019, January 31). *Five important classroom procedures.* Accessed at www .thoughtco.com/important-classroom-procedures-8409 on March 29, 2019.

Kletzien, S. B. (2009). Paraphrasing: An effective comprehension strategy. *The Reading Teacher, 63*(1), 73–77.

Kopan, T. (2018, March 5). *DACA's March 5 'deadline' marks only inaction.* Accessed at www.cnn.com/2018/03/05/politics/daca-deadline-march-5-passing-immigration -courts/index.html on May 21, 2019.

Korbey, H. (2017, October 27). *The power of being seen.* Accessed at www.edutopia .org/article/power-being-seen on March 29, 2019.

Landmark Outreach Staff. (2017). *Include students in the learning process.* Accessed at www.ldonline.org/article/65096 on March 29, 2019.

Linsin, M. (2015, January 10). *Why student modeling is so important.* Accessed at www .smartclassroommanagement.com/2015/01/10/why-student-modeling-is-so- important on May 28, 2019.

Martin, L. E., & Mulvihill, T. M. (2017). Current issues in teacher education: An interview with Dr. Linda Darling-Hammond. *The Teacher Educator, 52*(2), 75–83.

Marzano, R. J. (2011). The art & science of teaching / Making the most of instructional rounds. *Educational Leadership, 68*(5), 80–82.

Massey University. (2014, June 19). *Paraphrasing techniques.* Accessed at http://owll .massey.ac.nz/referencing/paraphrasing-techniques.php on May 28, 2019.

Master, A. (2015, August). *Praise that makes learners more resilient.* Accessed at http:// mindsetscholarsnetwork.org/wp-content/uploads/2015/09/Praise-That-Makes -Learners-More-Reslient.pdf on March 29, 2019.

McCarson, D. (n.d.). *Ideas and activities for teaching place value for the 2nd grade.* Accessed at https://education.seattlepi.com/ideas-activities-teaching-place-value -2nd-grade-3598.html on March 29, 2019.

McDowell, M. (2018, August 10). *How to create leveled success criteria.* Accessed at https://corwin-connect.com/2018/08/how-to-create-leveled-success-criteria on July 29, 2019.

McMillan, J. H., & Hearn, J. (2008). Student self-assessment: The key to stronger student motivation and higher achievement. *Educational Horizons, 87*(1), 40–49.

Meador, D. (2018, July 20). *Basic strategies for providing structure in the classroom.* Accessed at www.thoughtco.com/strategies-for-structure-in-the-classroom -4169394 on March 29, 2019.

Minigan, A. P. (2017, May 24). *The importance of curiosity and questions in 21st-century learning* [Blog post]. Accessed at http://blogs.edweek.org/edweek/global_ learning/2017/05/the_5th_c_curiosity_questions_and_the_4_cs.html on March 29, 2019.

Mirel, J., & Goldin, S. (2012, April 17). Alone in the classroom: Why teachers are too isolated. *The Atlantic.* Accessed at www.theatlantic.com/national/archive/2012/04 /alone-in-the-classroom-why-teachers-are-too-isolated/255976 on March 29, 2019.

Moss, C. M., & Brookhart, S. M. (2012). *Learning targets: Helping students aim for understanding in today's lesson.* Alexandria, VA: Association for Supervision and Curriculum Development. Accessed at www.ascd.org/ASCD/pdf/siteASCD /publications/books/learning-targets-sample-chapters.pdf on March 29, 2019.

Moss, C. M., Brookhart, S. M., & Long, B. A. (2011). Knowing your learning target. *Educational Leadership, 68*(6). Accessed at www.ascd.org/publications/educational -leadership/mar11/vol68/num06/Knowing-Your-Learning-Target.aspx on March 29, 2019.

National Council for Curriculum and Assessment. (2015). *Focus on learning: Learning intentions and success criteria.* Accessed at www.ncca.ie/media/1927/assessment -workshop-1_en.pdf on July 28, 2019.

National Governors Association Center for Best Practices & Council of Chief State School Officers. (2010a). *Common Core State Standards for English language arts and literacy in history/social studies, science, and technical subjects.* Washington, DC: Authors. Accessed at www.corestandards.org/assets/CCSSI_ELA%20Standards .pdf on September 10, 2019.

National Governors Association Center for Best Practices & Council of Chief State School Officers. (2010b). *Common Core State Standards for mathematics.* Washington, DC: Authors. Accessed at www.corestandards.org/assets/CCSSI_ Math%20Standards.pdf on October 2, 2019.

Neal, M. (2011). *Engaging students through effective questions.* Accessed at www .edcan.ca/articles/engaging-students-through-effective-questions on August 15, 2019.

The New Teacher Project. (2018). *The opportunity myth: What students can show us about how school is letting them down—and how to fix it.* Accessed at https:// opportunitymyth.tntp.org on July 30, 2019.

O'Dell, R. (2019, April 18). *Student opinion: Everyone deserves a chance. DACA should be preserved.* Accessed at https://newsela.com/read/preserve-daca/id/50747 on August 14, 2019.

Orens, S. (2018, March 23). *Students vote: Before the march, we let students vote on gun laws.* Accessed at https://newsela.com/read/students-vote-gun-control/id/41657 on August 14, 2019.

Palmer, P. J. (2007). *The courage to teach: Exploring the inner landscape of a teacher's life* (10th anniversary ed.). San Francisco: Jossey-Bass.

Pandolpho, B. (2018, July 12). *Strategies to help your students feel heard.* Accessed at www.edutopia.org/article/strategies-help-your-students-feel-heard on March 29, 2019.

PBIS Rewards. (n.d.). *5 simple ways to greet students*. Accessed at www.pbisrewards .com/blog/5-simple-ways-to-greet-students on March 29, 2019.

Power, B. (n.d.). *Talk in the classroom*. Accessed at www.scholastic.com/teachers /articles/teaching-content/talk-classroom on March 29, 2019.

ReadWorks. (2012). *American government—Preamble to the United States Constitution*. Accessed at www.readworks.org/article/American-Government---Preamble-to-the -United-States-Constitution/04c2c943-4634-49ae-bd73-c7954e4857f1 on August 14, 2019.

Richards, E. (n.d.). *The best and worst in praise*. Accessed at www.scholastic.com /teachers/articles/teaching-content/best-worst-praise on March 29, 2019.

Richardson, M. O. (2000). Peer observation: Learning from one another. *Thought & Action, 16*(1), 9–20.

Rimm-Kaufman, S., & Sandilos, L. (n.d.). *Improving students' relationships with teachers to provide essential supports for learning*. Accessed at www.apa.org/education/k12 /relationships.aspx on March 29, 2019.

Ripp, P. (2015). *Why are they disengaged? My students told me why*. Accessed at https:// pernillesripp.com/2015/09/06/why-are-they-disengaged-my-students-told-me -why on July 28, 2019.

Robertson, C. (2018, April 25). A lynching memorial is opening. The country has never seen anything like it. *The New York Times*. Accessed at www.nytimes. com/2018/04/25/us/lynching-memorial-alabama.html on May 21, 2019.

Rollins, S. P. (2015, November 15). *The precious first few minutes of class*. Accessed at www.teachthought.com/pedagogy/the-precious-first-few-minutes-of-class on March 29, 2019.

Rosen, M. (2016, July 12). *Strict gun laws ended mass shootings in Australia*. Accessed at www.sciencenewsforstudents.org/article/strict-gun-laws-ended-mass-shootings -australia on August 14, 2019.

Sawchuk, S. (2015, March 24). New studies find that, for teachers, experience really does matter. *Education Week*. Accessed at www.edweek.org/ew /articles/2015/03/25/new-studies-find-that-for-teachers-experience. html?r=691857876 on March 29, 2019.

Scheinfeld, D. R., Haigh, K. M., & Scheinfeld, S. J. P. (2008). *We are all explorers: Learning and teaching with Reggio principles in urban settings*. New York: Teachers College Press.

Scholastic. (n.d.). *Creating classroom routines and procedures: Best practices and pictures from real teachers' classrooms*. Accessed at http://teacher.scholastic.com/classroom_ management_pictures on March 29, 2019.

Schultz, M. (2015, March 6). *The importance of getting to know your students* [Blog post]. Accessed at www.bamradionetwork.com/edwords-blog/the-importance-of -getting-to-know-your-students on March 29, 2019.

Shabatu, J. (2018, March 5). *Bloom's taxonomy verb chart.* Accessed at https://tips.uark .edu/blooms-taxonomy-verb-chart on July 31, 2019.

Shakespeare, W. (1993). *Macbeth.* Mineola, NY: Dover.

Shapiro, E. S. (n.d.). *Tiered instruction and intervention in a response-to-intervention model.* Accessed at www.rtinetwork.org/essential/tieredinstruction/tiered -instruction-and-intervention-rti-model on August 1, 2019.

Sparks, S. D. (2013, May 31). Students can learn by explaining, studies say. *Education Week.* Accessed at www.edweek.org/ew/articles/2013/05/31/33aps.h32.html on March 29, 2019.

Stanford Alumni. (2014, October 9). *Developing a growth mindset with Carol Dweck* [Video file]. Accessed at https://youtu.be/hiiEeMN7vbQ on March 28, 2019.

Sue, D. W., Capodilupo, C. M., Torino, G. C., Bucceri, J. M., Holder, A. M. B., Nadal, K. L., et al. (2007). Racial microaggressions in everyday life: Implications for clinical practice. *American Psychologist, 62*(4), 271–286.

Taylor, J. (2009, September 3). *Parenting: Don't praise your children!* [Blog post]. Accessed at www.psychologytoday.com/us/blog/the-power-prime/200909 /parenting-dont-praise-your-children on March 29, 2019.

Terada, Y. (2018). *Welcoming students with a smile.* Accessed at https://www.edutopia .org/article/welcoming-students-smile on October 11, 2019.

Tomlinson, C. A. (2014). *The differentiated classroom: Responding to the needs of all learners* (2nd ed.). Alexandria, VA: Association for Supervision and Curriculum Development.

Tovani, C. (2011). *So what do they really know?: Assessment that informs teaching and learning.* Portland, ME: Stenhouse.

Truss, L. (2006). *Eats, shoots & leaves: Why, commas really do make a difference!* New York: Putnam's Sons.

Varlas, L. (2018). Why every class needs read alouds. *Education Update, 60*(1). Accessed at http://www.ascd.org/publications/newsletters/education-update/jan18 /vol60/num01/Why-Every-Class-Needs-Read-Alouds.aspx on August 15, 2019.

Wan, W. (2018, June 26). When we fight fire with fire: Rudeness can be as contagious as the common cold, research shows. *The Washington Post.* Accessed at www .washingtonpost.com/news/speaking-of-science/wp/2018/06/26/when-we-fight -fire-with-fire-rudeness-can-be-as-contagious-as-common-cold-research-shows on July 30, 2019.

Ward, R. (2018a, February 27). *Exploring the benefit mindset.* Accessed at www .edutopia.org/article/exploring-benefit-mindset on March 29, 2019.

Ward, R. (2018b, April 10). *The four crucial components of collaborative learning* [Blog post]. Accessed at https://rewardingeducation.wordpress.com/2018/04/10/the -four-crucial-components-of-collaborative-learning on March 29, 2019.

Ward, R. (2018c). *Talented teachers, empowered parents, successful students: Classroom strategies for including all families as allies in education.* Scotts Valley, CA: CreateSpace.

Weekly Reader. (2009). *Take care of our planet.* Accessed at www.readworks.org/article /Take-Care-of-Our-Planet/e24b98a5-0368-4654-8fb8-07b2119cf0cb# on August 21, 2019.

WestEd. (n.d.). *Chapter 2: Learning goals and success criteria—Activity 2.7.* Accessed at www.oregon.gov/ode/educator-resources/assessment/Documents/learning_goals_ success_criteria.pdf on March 29, 2019.

Wiggins, G. (2016, June 13). *Mandating the posting of learning targets and other mindless policies.* Accessed at www.teachthought.com/pedagogy/mandating -posting-of-learning-targets on March 29, 2019.

Wolpert-Gawron, H. (2016, August 11). *What the heck is inquiry-based learning?* Accessed at www.edutopia.org/blog/what-heck-inquiry-based-learning-heather -wolpert-gawron on August 1, 2019.

Wong, H. K., & Wong, R. T. (2018). *The first days of school: How to be an effective teacher* (5th ed.). Mountain View, CA: Wong.

Wyatt-Ross, J. (2018, June 28). *A classroom where everyone feels welcome.* Accessed at www.edutopia.org/article/classroom-where-everyone-feels-welcome on March 29, 2019.

Zeman, N. (2015). *What is our bad behavior teaching our kids?* Accessed at www .parents.com/parenting/better-parenting/style/what-is-our-bad-behavior-teaching -our-kids/ on July 30, 2019.

Zimmerman, B. J. (2001). Theories of self-regulated learning and academic achievement: An overview and analysis. In B. J. Zimmerman & D. H. Schunk (Eds.), *Self-regulated learning and academic achievement: Theoretical perspectives* (2nd ed., pp. 1–38). Mahwah, NJ: Erlbaum.

Index

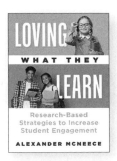

Loving What They Learn
Alexander McNeece

Deep learning and high engagement are possible for all students regardless of subject, grade, or previous experience. With *Loving What They Learn*, you will discover how to quantifiably measure needs and help students strengthen their academic self-concept and increase their self-efficacy.
BKF917

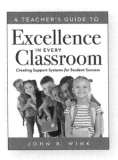

A Teacher's Guide to Excellence in Every Classroom
John R. Wink

Teachers today play a unique and significant role in the lives of their students. To support you in this important work, *A Teacher's Guide to Excellence in Every Classroom* outlines how to maximize your impact and unlock your students' full potential.
BKF895

Fifty Strategies to Boost Cognitive Engagement
Rebecca Stobaugh

Transform your classroom from one of passive knowledge consumption to one of active engagement. In this well-researched book, Rebecca Stobaugh shares 50 strategies for building a thinking culture that emphasizes essential 21st century skills—from critical thinking and problem-solving to teamwork and creativity.
BKF894

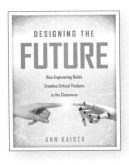

Designing the Future
Ann Kaiser

No matter the subject or grade, giving students engineering design challenges encourages creativity, communication, innovation, and collaboration. Throughout the book, you will find more than 25 easy-entry, low-risk engineering activities and projects you can begin immediately incorporating into existing classwork.
BKF853

Wait! Your professional development journey doesn't have to end with the last pages of this book.

We realize improving student learning doesn't happen overnight. And your school or district shouldn't be left to puzzle out all the details of this process alone.

No matter where you are on the journey, we're committed to helping you get to the next stage.

Take advantage of everything from **custom workshops** to **keynote presentations** and **interactive web and video conferencing**. We can even help you develop an action plan tailored to fit your specific needs.

Let's get the conversation started.

Call 888.763.9045 today.

SolutionTree.com